LIL' JOHN

Laughing My Way Through Life...

LIL' JOHN

Laughing My Way Through Life . . .

Stories from an Accidental Career on Cleveland TV—and More!

JOHN RINALDI

with C.R. Hendrix II

Gray & Company, Publishers
Cleveland

Photographs from the author's collection except as otherwise noted.

Gray & Company, Publishers
www.grayco.com

ISBN 978-1-59851-153-6
1

To my wife, Sherry.
I owe you a huge thanks. You not only survived many of the stories I'm about to tell, you stuck around long enough to hear me retell them—over and over again. I wouldn't want to share my life and all the laughs with anyone else.

To fans of the show.
If not for your support, The Big Chuck & Lil' John Show *wouldn't have existed. I have no idea where life would've taken me otherwise, but I'm certain it would've been a lot less fun.*

To my partner, Big Chuck.
What started as a single evening filming a skit in 1971 became a remarkable journey and a lifetime of adventure. The day you called you changed my life, and I am forever grateful.

CONTENTS

INTRODUCTION

Writing an autobiography demands intense self-discovery and reflection. You must meticulously examine your decisions, triumphs, and failures in order to offer readers an honest and compelling account of your journey and share the lessons you've learned along the way. Or . . . you can just wing it. That's what I did! If you came here seeking deep, thought-provoking insight, you bought the wrong book. This isn't *Chicken Soup for the Soul*; it's more like *Leftover Pizza for the Funny Bone.*

These are stories from growing up, from my TV years, and from navigating everyday life. Some people might say I wrote this book to talk about myself and to entertain myself. There is probably a kernel of truth in that! But the real reason is because I love making people laugh. By the end, I hope you will leave with a smile (or maybe wondering, *What is wrong with that guy?*).

Now that you know what to expect, come on in, gang—let's get acquainted!

I order my pizza with pepperoni and mushrooms, and my steak medium rare. I prefer summer over winter. I wish I had learned to swim. If I came with a warning sign, it would read, "Easily Combustible." If I had a superpower, I'd like to read minds. I never get tired of watching the original *Karate Kid* movie. I don't believe in ghosts. If I could travel back in time, I'd try to prevent world wars. I do not have any tattoos. I'm glad I was born in the twentieth century; otherwise, I might have been stuck as a court jester or cleaning up after horses in the streets.

A lot of people in Cleveland know me because I starred in a

hit local TV show—the longest-running of its kind (maybe you've heard of it). But I've done other things, too. I've wrestled bears, crashed in a hot-air balloon, bungee jumped, and walked along the edge of a building several stories up. I've been thrown through walls, handled snakes, and walked through a car wash. I've ridden motorcycles, raced cars, and owned several boats. I've been a circus ringmaster, played the bongos with Larry Holmes, and shared the stage with Tom Jones.

I've starred in a Super Bowl commercial and raised millions of dollars for charity. I've won several Emmys, sung on a Grammy-nominated record, and dressed as a woman more times than I can count. And now I've written a book! Let's see if it makes the bestseller list or ends up in the clearance bin.

It hasn't all been glamour and fun. I've been robbed several times, once at gunpoint. I've survived a car accident that should've killed me, lived through a hurricane, almost drowned, and even had a warrant put out for my arrest (yep, I was guilty). And that's just the first eighty years.

If you've learned enough already and want to stop reading, just a heads-up: there are no refunds. If you're still curious (or just a glutton for punishment), read on!

Writing this book made me realize that I wouldn't change a thing about my life. Every twist and turn led me right to where I am today. I've had enough fun to fill several lifetimes, but it's the people and the relationships in my life that have made the journey so special. I've been lucky to have an amazing family, loyal friends, and fantastic fans, and I am grateful for all of you.

I hope you enjoy walking down memory lane with me.

Oh, and before I forget, thank you for letting me into your bedroom every Friday night all those years—I promise, I didn't see a thing!

With heartfelt thanks,

Lil' John

WHERE SHOULD I START?

How About a Cliffhanger?

I wasn't scared, but I'll admit I was a little tense as I stood on top of the seventy-foot-tall platform looking down. The net that was supposed to catch me if the ropes failed seemed as small as a quarter. *If something goes wrong, there's no way I'll land on that thing*, I thought.

Then, just as I was about to jump, I heard one of the workers say to his partner, in the most casual tone, "Hey, isn't this strap supposed to be attached?"

"Oh, yeah—good thing you noticed," the other guy replied.

At that moment, my anxiety spiked. I didn't know what strap they were talking about, but I started frantically inspecting every piece of gear as if my life depended on it—which I was convinced it did.

Then came the final blow to my nerves: "Okay, Lil' John, remember—you have to dive headfirst."

My wife, Sherry, was watching from below. She didn't always come to these things, but she came this time because she was worried about this particular event. I'm sure she had our life insurance papers tucked in her purse just in case.

Now, if this isn't a literal cliffhanger, it's pretty darn close!

So how did I wind up in this situation? Believe it or not, it wasn't the first time—and it wouldn't be the last, either. It's all because of a local late-night TV show on which my partner and I showed monster movies and performed wacky skits for more than forty years. Well, that and my own lifelong habit of trying almost anything for a laugh. And . . . well, there's more to the story, and it takes some explaining. So maybe I should back up and start at the very beginning.

The Compound

It was a cold winter day in January 1946, and Michael and Anna Rinaldi were expecting their second child, John Anthony Rinaldi—yours truly! I arrived in St. Ann's Hospital and was taken home to East 110th Street, a Cleveland neighborhood of single- and multi-family homes. Although it was considered "inner city," it was a short distance from Cleveland's museums, the world-renowned Cleveland Clinic, and the prestigious Case Western Reserve University. I was an East Sider, which referred to anyone living east of the Cuyahoga River.

My older brother, Nick, and I shared a room; our sister, Marlene, had her own. We also had a dog. I would tell you his name, but I am not sure I can. About ten years ago, my wife and I were reminiscing, and I shared a story about our family dog, calling him by name. While chatting with my brother a few days later, I mentioned the story, but my brother called the dog by a different name. I called my sister to settle the matter; she had yet another name. Overhearing these conversations, my wife laughed. "None of you remember the name of your family dog?"

Both my parents came from large families. My mother had fourteen siblings, and my father had five. Many of them lived nearby. My immediate family and I lived on the first floor of a multi-family house. My Aunt Vera and her family occupied the upper floor. Next door lived my grandfather and more aunts and uncles. The front of their house was home to a small lemon ice shop. In a house at the front of our massive yard, my Aunt June lived on the top floor, and several suites on the lower floor were rented out to people who weren't part of the family. All of these relatives were on my mother's side. My grandfather owned the properties, and my family rented from him. I remember him complaining if any of us used too much water. Four-foot-high walls separated the yards, and I never thought twice before jumping over them to get to the next yard—regardless of the large drop on the other side or the fact that taking the sidewalk would've been easier.

My father's side of the family lived a few houses down. With so many relatives nearby, it felt like we lived within our own compound. I enjoyed having family nearby, but with so many eyes always watching—sometimes from their porch, sometimes from their kitchen window—it was hard to get away with anything.

Tiny Terror

My mother said I never gave her a moment's peace—it was a constant game of cat and mouse. She sometimes tied me to a chair for short periods so she could get the housework done. (People often gasp when I share that.) I was even more of a handful when we were out of the house together. At stores, I was constantly darting off and hiding, while my mother spent twenty minutes or more searching for me. Eventually, she tethered us together so I couldn't run away (but let's not call it a leash).

The idea of being "grounded" didn't exist for us kids. We got spanked. The worst words we could hear were, "Wait until your father gets home." And that was after our mother had already spanked us. But we wouldn't make it easy for our parents; we became moving targets. I remember hiding under the bed once while my mother did her best to prod me out with the mop handle.

Early Days

I grew up in a time very much like the one portrayed in the movie *A Christmas Story,* when the world was simpler and lifestyles were modest, with fewer frills than today. Kids were tight-knit and ruled the streets, and neighbors knew each other and looked out for one another. It was an unspoken rule that if a child misbehaved, any nearby adult had the authority to set them straight.

Specialty shops—corner stores, drugstores, butchers—were within walking distance. For luxury items and non-essentials, like clothes, jewelry, or toys, downtown was where we went. Cleveland had a great mix of department stores and retail shopping—Sterling-Lindner, Halle's, Higbee's, May Company, Woolworth's, and Kresge's. A trip downtown with the entire family was a big event, with one of the highlights being a visit to the top of the Terminal Tower, a real adventure for ten-year-old me.

Those stores put up incredible window displays to draw people inside, and come the holidays, those windows turned into magical wonderlands filled with toys. Two of my favorite childhood toys were little green plastic army men and cap guns. I recall spending many Saturdays playing cops and robbers, cowboys and Indians. I didn't mean to hit my cousin so hard on the head with the butt of my gun, but that's what I saw on TV when someone resisted going to jail. It's been a long time since those make-believe days, but I still love war stories, westerns, and true crime, and I'm an avid reader of books on these subjects today.

Christmas was always a festive occasion, and I was focused on the gifts waiting under the tree. But as the years passed, I realized the real gift was being surrounded by family. Looking back, I can see that those gatherings defined what the holidays still mean to me today. Christmas Eve was spent with my father's

My father, brother, and sister, and me—all dressed up for Easter. Along with my mother, we lived on the first floor of a multi-family house surrounded by relatives on Cleveland's East Side.

side of the family; Christmas Day belonged to my mother's side. But no matter whose house we were in, the experience was the same: lively conversations, a joyful kind of chaos that only a big extended family can create, and the unmistakable smell of food drifting through the air.

Some memories stick out in my mind as if they happened only yesterday. We had a four-foot-tall Christmas tree that we proudly placed on top of a three-foot-high table so it looked as grand as possible. When the season was over, the whole thing—lights, ornaments, and all—went straight into a giant plastic bag, ready for next year. I remember waiting impatiently for my uncle Edward to finish work and show up for the festivities. He always arrived late. I have very little to critique about my father, but he needed help when it came to my mother's Christmas gift. Every year, she opened a pair of pajamas. But worse, it was the same set from the previous year, rewrapped. That was the entire gift. It wasn't until we kids were old enough to realize this was a problem that we convinced him to get her something else.

Radio was the main form of home entertainment. Televisions were a luxury primarily for the wealthy. However, my uncle Edward was a doctor and had the financial means to buy televisions for all his brothers, so our family had one before most. Early TVs had small screens—about the size of the TV trays we ate our meals on—and were so heavy that moving them took at least two strong men. By 1955, television had become common in most homes. I didn't watch much TV, but when I did, it was mostly westerns and combat movies. One of my favorite shows was the very popular *Captain Video and His Video Rangers*, the first science fiction program on television. It's ironic that I found success performing on television, considering how little interest I had in it while growing up.

I used to go with my mother to shop for groceries at open-air markets near downtown. They were similar to the farmers' markets that are around today. Our favorite was Central Market, located on the property that became the Gateway sports complex, including Progressive Field and Rocket Arena. I learned which vendors offered the best goods by watching my mother, and by age ten I was responsible for grocery shopping, making solo bus trips to the market. My mother wrote a grocery list for me, which I took to the vendors. Customers didn't haggle over price, but they did haggle over which item they wanted. "I don't want the oranges on the top; I want those on the left, near the bottom." Once the vendors knew you as a regular customer, you got the best stuff without asking. I placed the groceries in leather shopping bags I had brought with me, carried the bags to the bus stop, dropped them off, and returned to the market for another load. When I finished, the bus driver would help me load the bags onto the bus for the ride home. When I got to my stop, adult passengers would help me unload my haul. Then, I'd leave the bags at the bus stop and walk home to get a wagon for the final leg of the journey. It's hard to imagine today, but back then, no one messed with my bags. It's even harder to imagine today parents sending a child alone into the city.

Tuesdays, Thursdays, and Sundays were pasta nights in our house. On Mondays, we had soup; Wednesdays and Saturdays, meat dishes. My mom was a good cook, but baking wasn't her strong suit—except for bread and pizza. She made those weekly, and they were always delicious. It wasn't until I went to college that I ever tasted store-bought bread.

In addition to grocery shopping, I was assigned the dreaded task of retrieving our garbage cans after the garbage truck came and emptied them. I didn't have to take the full cans to the curb because they were too heavy for me, but every Saturday morning I dragged and banged all thirteen filthy but empty cans back to their resting place—making as much noise as possible. The clatter of the cans served as a signal announcing the start of the day. If I had to be up early on a Saturday, so did everyone else in the neighborhood. You might wonder why there were so many garbage cans. Remember, many family members lived in houses next door, and I was responsible for all the cans for the entire compound.

Thanks to my grandfather on my mother's side, our family learned how to make wine. Every year, he organized a two-day event, with crates of grapes delivered to kick things off. He had all the necessary equipment in the basement—barrels, buckets, bottles, and a winepress. He would carefully blend the right combination of red and white grapes, and then it was up to the rest

Me and our four-foot-tall Christmas tree (which turned into a seven-footer on the table). I still love cowboy movies and books. Oddly enough, considering my eventual career, TV wasn't a big part of my childhood.

of us to take over. Each of us had a role: some turned the grapes, others loaded them, my brother crushed them; my job was to haul the empty crates to the trash and clean up. Our efforts yielded several barrels of wine, which my grandfather would serve at family gatherings throughout the year. We kids had the important job of tapping the barrel and filling the bottles for those gatherings. God help us if we spilled any—Grandpa was adamant that not a single drop be wasted after all that work. I fondly remember eating dinner with my grandpa, especially when he got older. He would sit at the table sipping Old Grand-Dad whiskey—that was his drink, aside from the wine he made—while eating fish. He'd pick that fish so clean that by the end of dinner, it looked like one of those cartoon fish with just the bones left.

It's funny how some of the most seemingly obscure and random things stick out as memories from childhood. One morning I was sent to the top floor of the front house to get milk from my Aunt June. Keep in mind that milk came in glass bottles then. On my way back, I tripped and tumbled down the steep wooden steps, landing hard at the bottom. Somehow, the glass jar of milk I was holding remained entirely intact. As I lay there, stunned and banged up, my grandfather started clapping as if I'd just performed a perfect gymnastics routine.

We Played and We Hustled

We were never poor, but we were far from wealthy, so extravagant vacations and frequent dining out were not part of my childhood. Despite life's simplicity, though, something was always happening in the neighborhood. One memorable event was the semi-annual rat eradication. Living in the city meant dealing with these pesky rodents, and twice a year, we cleared them out. A mixture of ginger ale and gasoline was placed out as bait, and when the rats gathered to drink, my uncle would light the concoction and . . . KABOOM! The following day, we'd clean up the remains with shovels. As grim as that might sound, just a few blocks away, a store processed and sold chicken. It was a common sight to see chickens having their throats cut and being tossed into a plucking machine. Despite its starkness, that didn't bother me; it was simply a part of the life I knew, where people did what they needed to survive.

I didn't grow up with modern household luxuries like air conditioning. In the summer, we often stayed out late into the evening, waiting for the house to cool down to a temperature below that of a pizza oven. One of our favorite late-night pastimes was sitting on the curb, watching for drunks stumbling out of the neighborhood bar. Sometimes, they'd drop loose change, and we'd scramble to grab it. With some luck and fast reflexes, our loot would treat us to ice cream the next day.

There was no such thing as an allowance, so earning money was a necessity. Cleveland had three newspapers then—the *Plain Dealer* in the morning and the *Cleveland Press* and *Cleveland News* in the afternoon. I delivered the *Press* to forty-two customers. In the summer, my friends always wanted to play baseball right after school, so I recruited them to help with my paper deliveries, telling them that way I could play sooner. Five of us would get the work done in no time at all. Even now, I could still navigate my old paper route without much trouble, especially my first customer of the day—my grandpa. His paper had to be delivered first, on time, at the same time every day. On cold winter days, he'd hand me a small cough medicine bottle filled with wine and say, "Here, this will keep you warm. And don't tell your mother." Years later, my mom admitted she never understood why I always came home in such a good mood after delivering the newspapers.

Even when I had money, I spent much of my spare time doing things for free. During the winter, I would go ice skating with friends at Woodland Hills Park. (It was renamed Luke Easter Park in the 1980s.) When I was older, I'd meet girlfriends there to skate and hold hands. I was a good skater, but I never quite got the hang of backward skating. I spent countless hours playing one sport or another. One of my favorite games was Wiffle Ball, and I still recall the house rules. My grandfather had a chair parked right where we played. If you hit the chair, you were out automatically. But if he was sitting in it? Game over. No discussion and no arguing—we'd scatter like cockroaches. Because we were in the city, football and baseball games were sometimes played in the streets, where sewer caps and water inlets served as bases and end zone markers. Timeouts were called long enough to let cars pass by.

In addition to the neighborhood pickup games, there was also an organized baseball league. But unlike today's youth sports, which parents and volunteers meticulously organize, the kids handled everything. We formed our teams and took the bus to the recreation center at city hall to register for the summer game schedule. Once all the teams were registered, the city sent out a schedule to the players. Kids managed the games entirely, with kid umpires and coaches—never a parent. The only aspect with any adult involvement was reporting the final score to the city. We were even responsible for our uniforms. Each player bought a white T-shirt and letters from the dry goods store, and moms would iron on the team name. My team was called the "Temples," after the Cleveland Indians' second baseman, Johnny Temple. I still remember a childhood dream so vivid it's stuck with me all these years: I had a magic pill that made me unstoppable at any sport. I could score a touchdown on every drive and hit a home run with every swing. But there was a catch: I only had 100 pills, so the coaches couldn't use me all the time; they had to save me for the winning play.

Two-Wheeled Freedom

Kids were expected to be outdoors unless they were eating or doing schoolwork. On the weekends, we'd leave the house early, come back for lunch, and be gone again until dark. Most kids had to be home when the streetlights came on, but not me. My dad could whistle like a freight train, and when he did, I dropped whatever I was doing and ran home for dinner. Unfortunately, I didn't inherit that skill. So when my kids were little, I used an air horn.

Kids of my generation spent a lot of time on their bikes. I learned to ride quickly; otherwise, it meant a lot of hard falls in our all-brick yard. Most kids in the neighborhood had a bike; those who didn't were left out of many adventures. Our bikes were more than just a means of getting around—they were our tickets to freedom. Our only limitation when we left home was how far we wanted to ride. Some of my favorite destinations were the Sears store at East 86th Street and Carnegie Avenue, and Western Auto Parts to get bike supplies. Of course, no ride was complete without stopping at the neighborhood store for pop or snacks. My friends and I never rode downtown—we figured our bikes would get stolen there. We spent many summer days at the Shaker Lakes in Shaker Heights. We washed our bikes with the lake water.

One of our regular summer adventures occurred at the community garden on Buckeye Road and East 116th Street, about three miles from home. We were given small plots in which to grow vegetables. We ended up with so much produce that we sold the extras. Behind the library, tables and scales were set up, and we were given a list of fair prices. This was so we wouldn't get taken advantage of by the neighborhood hagglers. If we weren't biking to the garden, we'd walk—but never the boring, straight route. Instead, we'd make a game of it by cutting through St. Luke's Hospital. We'd sneak in through an exit door, head to the second floor, climb out onto a balcony, shimmy down a tree to the first floor, pop back into the hospital, and stroll through the emergency room on our way out. We never caused trouble, so no one ever stopped us.

Italian Roots, American Life

Both sets of my grandparents came from the same region in Italy before immigrating to the U.S. My parents were both in the first generation of their families born here, and they grew up in the same Cleveland neighborhood.

My mother's siblings were spaced so far apart in age that her oldest sister could have been her mother. Before getting married, my mother worked at the food counter at Woolworth's downtown, earning forty-two cents an hour plus tips. After getting married, she stepped into the role of homemaker, as was typical for women of her generation. And let me tell you, if you've ever heard the phrase, "You could eat off the floor," that saying originated in our house. My mother didn't just clean; she scared germs out of the house. Our house was not only clean but also orderly, with nothing out of place. I am sure my own neatness came from her. Although she was always busy with the house and cooking, my mother enjoyed spending time with us and the other kids in the neighborhood. She took us trick-or-treating and to the movies when she had the money. Neither of my parents helped with homework, but they made sure we did it, and both were active PTA members. Back then, PTA meetings were standing-room-only. (Sadly, crickets outnumber parents in some school systems now.)

My father grew up in the inner city. He attended Brownell School on Brownell Street, later renamed East 14th Street. The school eventually became the first campus of Cuyahoga Community College. Even at a young age, my father often held multiple jobs. (No surprise, I was the same way as an adult.) He ultimately spent most of his adult life as an electrical inspector for the city, but he also worked as a bellhop at the Hollenden Hotel downtown. It was regarded as one of the finest hotels in Cleveland. Presidents, pro athletes, and celebrities frequently stayed there. My dad struck up a friendship with Babe Ruth, the New York Yankees All-Star, who stayed at the hotel when he was in town. The Babe would tip my father two dollars and give him several signed baseballs, which he could sell or give to friends and family.

Family was at the heart of my father's life, but his friendships held a special place right beside it. He had a tight group from childhood, and those friendships lasted his entire life. Their friendship ran so deep that they collectively purchased a plot of land on East Boulevard at East 116th Street and built the Monarch Club. This clubhouse became a hub of their social lives—hosting everything from club meetings to family picnics and holiday gatherings. Some of my earliest and fondest memories were of family gatherings there. The Monarch Club was also a stage for their creativity. My father and his friends put on comedy shows for the public, with my father often taking the spotlight as the comic or the wise-ass. His role as a showman was a defining part of his personality and a trait I undoubtedly inherited. One of his memorable antics was as a corner man for a local wrestler. He'd jump into the ring and start teasing the wrestlers, which was hilarious. Whenever they hit him, he'd roll across the canvas, and the crowd loved it. My father's short stature amplified the laughter compared to the wrestlers' large size.

My father was short like me. I'm not sure how far back small stature runs in my family, but the height differences among some of my relatives are striking. My grandfather, whom I never met, was 6′5″, while my grandmother stood at just 3′11″. My father never let his height hold him back, and he successfully passed this outlook on to me. He often said things like, "Do your feet touch the ground? Then you're as tall as you need to be," or "Just keep going and have a good time." Another favorite of his was, "It's a big man's world; go get in it." And that's precisely what I did. From him, I learned that my height should never be a barrier, and it never was.

Surprisingly, I didn't even realize I was short until others pointed it out during my early youth. In stark contrast to my father's perspective, my uncle, Dr. Edward Rinaldi—who was also of smaller stature—held a different perspective. When I was very young, he gave me some perplexing advice: not to have children. Puzzled, I asked him why. He responded, "The only way to get rid

My father, Mike Rinaldi, working as a bellhop at the Hollenden Hotel, one of the finest hotels in Cleveland. He often held multiple jobs. No surprise, I was the same way as an adult.

of small kids is to stop having them." Despite his brilliance as a doctor, my uncle was self-conscious about his height.

My father always stayed up waiting for us kids to come home, no matter how late it was. I remember coming home late one night, and he asked why I hadn't called. I explained that I couldn't reach the phone to put in the dime. He replied, "You got a mouth, don't you? Use it." His guidance not to let any obstacle—not just height—hold me back became a big part of how I would live my life.

I've long realized just how much I am like my father and how much he has influenced me. Even when my wife and I disagree, she'll say, "Listen, Mike," a direct nod to my father, using his name. It reminds me of how his traits and ways are woven into my life. His spirit of friendship, talent for entertaining, and positive outlook have shaped who I am today. (By the way Dad, even though you always said, "They are not going to lower the curbs, so step up," today, curbs have been lowered to accommodate disabled people.

One of the most amusing stories I remember about my father was when he came home one evening, clearly upset about something he didn't want to discuss. After some coaxing, he finally opened up. "I just saw my birth certificate and learned I was born in 1909," he said. "I always thought I was born in 1910. I'm a year older now—I've lost a year of my life!"

SCHOOL DAYS

Mr. Popular

Anthony Wayne Elementary School was about six blocks from my house. The local Catholic school was another half a block away. All the kids walked to school together, but we eventually split up depending on which school we attended. The public-school kids had an hour for lunch, so we'd walk home, eat, and have a snowball fight on the way back to school. We teased the Catholic school kids because they couldn't leave for lunch. But after school, we all gathered again as if none of it mattered.

All the school crossing guards were kids working with about as much supervision as our neighborhood baseball leagues. I desperately wanted to be out there waving a flag like a pint-sized traffic cop, but because of my height, the school was worried a driver wouldn't see me, and I'd get flattened by a passing car. So, instead, I was given the prestigious title of Crossing Guard Captain. My sole responsibility was making sure the other guards were where they were supposed to be.

After school, I attended many classes at the local community center we called "the neighborhood house." My cousin Dolores and I took tap dancing classes. I picked it up quickly. There are ten basic steps to tap dancing, and I can still remember a few of them. Classes kept us busy—one day, it was tap dancing; the next, boxing; and another might be basket weaving. I performed in many school plays. Whenever the director needed that extra "wow" factor, I was asked to join the cast. Although I wasn't always thrilled about committing to weeks of rehearsals, I enjoyed performing. One of those plays was about King Arthur, and I played Arthur. We made all the props ourselves, and of course, no elementary school play is complete without something going hilariously wrong. When the big moment arrived for me to pull the sword from the stone, it wouldn't budge. I pulled with all my might—until I had no choice but to lift the entire paper-mache rock along with the sword over my head, claiming my rightful place as king. The crowd roared with laughter—a sound I'd grow to know well, and love.

Junior High

Audubon Junior High School, which included 7th, 8th, and 9th grades, was about a mile away from home. Most kids walked, but my cousin and I didn't—we hitchhiked! Back then, thumbing a ride with a stranger was a common form of public transportation. Our school schedule was so routine that we got picked up by the same driver almost every day to and from school. At Christmas, my mom baked cookies to thank our unofficial chauffeur. When kids couldn't get a ride in the winter, or just for fun, we would "boot hop," grabbing onto the bumper of an unsuspecting car and sliding along the snow-covered streets for a free ride.

It was during junior high that I realized how popular I was and how large my circle of friends had become. There was a contest to elect a class king and queen, and the voting process involved dropping money into jars: each penny counted as a vote, and the jar with the most money won the title. My jar was nearly full when it was stolen the day before the votes were counted. The news spread quickly, and by the next day, before the vote, my jar was refilled and I won by a landslide. I remember the counselor saying, "You've got something, John—how the kids rallied to refill your jar. You won't have any problems when you get to high school."

Growing up, every year, I got a new suit: one jacket with two pairs of pants. I kept wearing nice suits throughout my jewelry-business career—and ruined a few of them in my TV career!

Ruling the High School Halls

I entered John Adams High School as a freshman in 1961. It was a big leap from junior high—more people and much more freedom, especially with friends who could drive. High school was still very traditional in the early 1960s, but things were beginning to feel different from the 1950s. The civil rights movement was gaining momentum and kids questioned authority more. Television was growing in popularity, and rock music was everywhere. Motown and the Beach Boys were among my favorites. One of the highlights of the local music scene was *The Big 5 Show*, a musical variety show that aired in Cleveland from 1964 to 1971 on Channel 5 at 5 p.m. It was renamed *Upbeat* when it went national in 1965. The show featured live musical acts, including big names like the Beatles. Occasionally, the production crew would come to our school dances and invite students to come to the TV studio and appear on the show. While my friends and I were all good dancers, we were never interested in it.

I didn't date much in high school, and for school events my friends and I typically went together, boys and girls. The boy who drove to the event would get the honor of taking the girls home at the end of the night, which usually involved a stop at Manners Big Boy along the way. One evening, my buddy and I were taking a couple of girls home when our car broke down. It was just our bad luck that some other guys drove up and offered the girls a ride, leaving us stuck alone with the broken-down car.

Other kids' growth spurts in high school made it hard for me to compete in sports, and I was never good enough to make any of the school teams. Instead, I maintained excellent grades and held many student-elected positions, including Key Club secretary, president of the radio club, president of the student congress, and last but not least, class president. In the class president election, I ran against the school's star athlete. Only three people voted against me—one was the other candidate's sister. I was also held in high regard by the school staff. Because of that, I could write a note for friends saying, "Please excuse Dave from class; I need him. John Rinaldi," and students would be released without question.

Tough Boys, Rough Boys

In the previous two decades, the country had gone through World War II and the Korean War, and by the time I entered high school, the war in Vietnam was in full swing. The Cold War with the Soviet Union remained a constant threat. My elementary school, like many others at that time, issued military-style ID tags for identification in case of nuclear attacks. High school boys were expected to be physically fit, and gym classes focused on developing strength and endurance, preparing young men for military service. On the first day of class, the gym teacher, who we thought was old but who was still in great shape for being in his fifties, said, "You young guys are all full of energy, and now is the time to get some of that out of your system. If any of you want to take a swing at me, come on up. I won't hold anything against you." As we whispered about how we could beat him in a fight, the gym doors swung open and in walked other gym instructors carrying baseball bats—tough guys who meant business. "But before you come up," our teacher continued, "I brought some friends along."

Our senior gym class, which was called "Commando," was held every day and often outdoors, rain or shine. Tuesdays were grueling Marine challenges like endless push-ups and half-mile runs. Thursdays were for self-defense classes and sparring with partners, using boxing or wrestling techniques. Sometimes the gym teacher would join in and battle two students at once. Sometimes two smaller students would face the biggest guy in class, who would be handicapped by being made to hop on one foot or fight with one arm behind his back. As a rite of passage, everyone who completed Commando class earned a swat on the behind with a paddle along with a commemorative paper patch to pin on their shirt.

If you find these stories hard to believe, let me tell you one more. A three-round boxing match was scheduled between a student and the gym teacher, all sparked by a disagreement. The fight took place in the school gym, and it seemed that the entire student body had shown up to watch. One might think the older gym teacher had the upper hand, but the student was no slouch; he was in the Golden Gloves program and had skills of his own.

They duked it out for a few rounds, but no real damage was done. Ultimately, they left the ring as friends, having settled their differences in a manner considered shocking by today's standards. The most incredible part? No one gave a second thought to this kind of physical confrontation.

These stories may seem strange today, but we were being prepared for the military. I suspect some of our tough school training probably saved some lives.

Gym class was scheduled in the morning for two reasons. One was that some students didn't have regular access to bathing at home and kids were required to shower after class. Some kids brought towels they only took home at the end of the school year, and by then they were beyond disgusting. Thankfully, my mother insisted that we bring our towels home every week to be laundered. The second reason was that fighting was common in those days, and the school believed that by wearing us out early, we would be too exhausted to get into trouble later in the day, particularly around lunchtime, when most fights occurred. If wearing us out in the gym didn't work, teachers had various other methods for keeping us in line, including corporal punishment. On the first day of school, one of the teachers asked ten boys to come to the front of the class during study hall. He gave each a swat with a paddle and said, "That's for doing nothing; imagine what it'll be if you do something bad." The last thing any kid wanted to do was tell their parents they got paddled. Back then, the teacher was always right, and a kid faced additional punishment at home.

Fighting wasn't unusual back then, and when kids came home with a black eye or a few bruises, parents didn't raise an eyebrow. I was only ever in one fight growing up. While I could hold my own, I never liked fighting, so early on I came up with a plan to avoid it altogether. In class, students were usually seated in alphabetical order, but I purposefully sat in the middle of four girls, one in each corner. When a fight broke out, the girls would

My circle of friends grew steadily throughout my school years. In high school I held several student-elected positions, including president of the student congress and class president. Does that sweater look familiar? It was a popular style.

naturally stand up, and no boy was ever going to hit or shove a girl aside to get to me. Despite my efforts, confrontations couldn't be entirely avoided. One day, some friends and I got into a scuffle with another student. It should have been a minor incident and quickly forgotten, but things took a turn when one of the students accidentally cut his arm on a locker. As a result, the school sent all of us for counseling. We had to take a city bus to the board of education office during school hours to see a psychiatrist.

"I'm not crazy," I told the doctor.

"Whoa!" he responded, "You can't use that word.' "

Later in our session he asked, "When you saw the blood from the cut, did any thoughts pop into your head?"

"Thoughts? What kind of thoughts? He accidentally cut his arm on the locker door."

We had to keep seeing that doctor for three weeks before he concluded we weren't crazy. Sorry, doc, I used that word again.

Homework and Hard Work

We used to cruise around Cleveland in my buddy Chuck's '48 Ford. The passenger door of that old car wouldn't latch properly and would fly open on corners unless held shut. I always joked that if we ever got in an accident, I'd fall out and we could retire on the big cash settlement. Believe it or not, we actually did get into an accident—and I damn near broke my shoulder banging on the door trying to get out because it wouldn't open!

Working and earning money have always been a part of my life, including high school. When I was seventeen, Chuck would pick me up after school on Thursdays in that '48 Ford and drive me to my friend Carol's house. I stayed with her family Thursday through Sunday because it was a short walk from where I worked (I didn't drive at the time). They became like my second family. They even fed me. I'd grab a little sleep in the evening; then someone would wake me up around 10:30 p.m. so I could make my 11:00 p.m. shift.

I worked Thursday, Friday, and Saturday nights for a business monitoring police scanners in Cleveland and surrounding communities. The office was filled with scanners. The gig was simple: If I heard about an emergency, such as a house fire, I'd dispatch one of our salesmen to the location to provide a repair quote. One night, I heard about a mugging at an address that sounded familiar. Then I realized it was my office location! I looked out

That's me on the right, age sixteen, with friends during summer. How about those muscles? High school boys were expected to be physically fit, and our gym classes sometimes seemed like military training. I still had great hair back then, too!

the window and saw a lady being assaulted. Fortunately, within seconds, the police showed up. I was working Friday and Saturday nights but because I didn't want to miss out on all the fun my friends were having, I'd invite some of them to the office to keep me company. I could still hear the radios, and if a call came in, I'd tell everyone to quiet down. Employees weren't supposed to sleep on the job, but I could manage a few cat naps each night and that was all I needed.

High school was a blast and the time flew by. At graduation, I was seated in the front row along with the National Honor Society members. When an announcement called for the members to stand, everyone in the first row stood—except for me. I wasn't one of them. My smart-ass friend leaned over and said, "Look who's

Delivering the 1964 January commencement speech at John Adams High School. "Who's standing now, smart-ass?"

still sitting, Rinaldi." But then they called for the class president to stand. I rose and said, "Who's the only one standing now, smart-ass?" Our school held two graduation ceremonies each year—one in January and another in June. I graduated in January, which allowed me to start classes at Ohio State University in the spring quarter rather than waiting until the fall, as most incoming students do.

I was part of the prom committee, and years later I also held that role for our tenth-year and fiftieth-year reunions. At our tenth reunion, I announced, "I am not sure we are going to have another one of these. We were idiots then, and we are idiots now." That got a big laugh from the crowd. Two of my female classmates were also on the planning committee. These two ladies did an exceptional job and they were no wallflowers. Several people showed up without tickets to our tenth reunion, claiming they just wanted to come in for a few minutes to say hello to specific individuals. The girls turned them away. Fast-forward forty years to our fiftieth reunion, and here came the same freeloaders with the same story and still no ticket.

LIFE AS A BUCKEYE

Settling in to Baker

With high school behind me, I was on to my next adventure: College. Everyone in my family who attended college went to Ohio State University, so there was never any doubt about where I would go. For a major, I chose business, and I eventually focused in on marketing. I'd love to say I had a grand plan when selecting a marketing major, but one reason was that it was the only major that didn't require studying a foreign language.

I got off to a rocky start. When I went to pick up my class schedule, one of the faculty members thought I was an underage kid who had wandered in off the street, and he almost threw me out. Next up was a less-than-encouraging orientation. We were lined up and told to look to our left, then our right. The message? "Two out of three of you won't graduate." (Despite these words of encouragement, the guy next to me earned his PhD in four years, and the guy on the other side got his in five.)

It was my first time living away from home, and I felt a sense of independence. Baker Hall, my residence, was divided down the middle: the cafeteria was centrally located, with the boys' dorms on one side and the girls' dorms on the other. As I settled in, it didn't take long for college chaos to kick in. The drinking age then was eighteen for beer and twenty-one for liquor. Many students preferred drinking liquor, so I devised a clever scheme to assist my peers by selling whiskey shots from my dorm room. Today, this would be called a "side hustle." My resident advisor, or RA, had a hunch I was up to something and tried everything to catch me, but never did. My room had a big dresser with a mirror and a cabinet that stretched all the way to the ceiling. Behind that cabinet was a hole in the wall—perfect for hiding liquor. I kept the bottle in a laundry bag tied to a rope, which hung from a nail behind the wall. I also sold pop, which I stored in the window during winter to keep it cold.

It Wasn't All Studying

One of the perks of being unusually short was that nobody ever asked for my ID. I guess people didn't want to risk offending the little guy. So, not only could I easily buy liquor for my dorm room "speakeasy," but I could also stroll into any bar and drink without any questions. Before I turned 21, I was a regular at a local campus bar and became good friends with the owner. On my 21st birthday, I strutted in, proudly placed my ID on the bar, and ordered a drink. The owner picked up my license, saw my birth date, stared at me in disbelief. "You son of a bitch!" he blurted, before throwing me out for that night.

My friends and I were constantly bending the rules. Our dorm held a Christmas decorating contest, with a fifty-dollar budget and a pizza party prize for the winners. We decided there were better ways to spend fifty dollars than on decorations, but we still wanted to win the contest. Nearby was a Christmas tree lot perched on the edge of a steep ravine. My friends and I bought two trees. Then we came back late that night, after closing, to gather a couple more trees that had mysteriously fallen into the ravine. We won the contest by cutting our trees in half, length-wise, attaching them to our doors, and decorating them with odds and ends we found for free. I've always believed that if three people know a secret, you have to eliminate two of them to ensure it remains a secret. With about fifteen of us in on the stunt, it wasn't long before the judges found out, and we were disqualified.

Poker, euchre, and canasta—we played them all in college. One night around 3 a.m., we were in the lounge playing poker for money—nickels, dimes, and pennies. The RA caught us in the act and issued pink slips to everyone, which meant we had to see the dorm director. I quickly came up with a plan for the group. "Tell the dorm director that we weren't gambling; we were only using the money because we didn't have poker chips, and everyone got their money back at the end of the night. We won't get into trouble if we all tell the same story." That's what we did, and while it was obvious that the director didn't believe a word, he let us go with just a warning.

We moved our games from the public lounge into one of the dorm rooms. During another late-night gambling session, there was a knock at the door. No one ever locked their doors—mainly because we didn't have anything valuable to steal, and also because the dorm had strict rules that only allowed someone to enter if they were verbally invited. All we had to do was be quiet, but one of my idiot friends blurted out, "Come in." I immediately dove under the bed out of sight. Once again, the RA gave everyone (except me, this time) a pink slip. I told my friends they should stick to our old story. One of my friends ratted me out, so I was summoned to meet the dorm director along with everyone else. The dorm director, who was also a friend, said, "Tell me the truth, John—were you at the game?"

"Am I speaking to my friend or the dorm director?" I asked.

"The dorm director."

I replied with purposely flawed logic: "I didn't get a pink slip, so I must not have been there."

* * *

I met Dick when I first arrived on campus, and we hit it off instantly. We were inseparable. Dick was a great pool player, and although I didn't play, I hung out at the pool halls with him. Everyone at school knew how good he was, so they wouldn't play him for money. If Dick wanted to get some side action, we went downtown to the pool hall. Once Dick got a game going, there was always the question of who would hold the money. Dick would suggest, "Let the little guy hold it, he's always here." No one knew Dick and I were together because I'd enter and leave the pool hall separately from him. Our deal was that if Dick lost, I'd pay the money, but if he won and a fight broke out, I'd take off with the cash.

I was a bit of a hustler as well. I was in excellent physical shape and could easily do one hundred one-armed push-ups, either arm, or more than two hundred two-arm push-ups. I would bet guys much bigger than me that I could do twice as many one-armed push-ups as they could do with two arms, and I never lost. We often went out to the parking lot for the challenge, and I always remembered to wipe away any gravel or debris before hitting the pavement, which gave me an advantage.

Dick was on the wrestling team, and he suggested I try out for team manager. I wasn't a typical manager doing grunt work; instead, I told the wrestlers, "I'm not your mother; pick up your own towels." When the team traveled, the wrestlers had to be in bed early, but there was no such rule for the coaches—or the manager. One night in Chicago, one of the trainers and I took the elevated train downtown to the Playboy Club. After eating and having a drink, we hopped back on the train to return to our hotel. I had heard it wasn't a good idea to take the L at midnight, and now I understood why. I don't think there was a passenger on there who wasn't drunk, high, or crazy. I couldn't wait to get off that train.

Woody Hayes

Our dorm building had a complex phone system. Visitors who called from the lobby could easily dial into a student's room. However, if a call came from an outside line, it had to go through a switchboard first. The switchboard operator would then ring your room, letting you know you had a call to be picked up on the hall phone. Students would race down the hall, hoping no one was already using the phone. If the phone on your floor was already in use, you'd have to sprint to another floor. When I first arrived at school, I roomed with two other guys who were both named John. When a call came in for John, we all ran down the hall. By the end of the quarter, we usually knew who was getting the call.

I lived next door to Steve Hayes, son of the legendary OSU football coach Woody Hayes. Woody coached the Buckeyes for nearly thirty years, winning several national championships and Big Ten titles. Occasionally, Woody would come by the dorm and call Steve's room. I was often in Steve's room and answered the phone. Woody would say, "John, would you tell Steve his father, W. W. Hayes, is downstairs?" I always found it odd that he specified his full name; it's not as if Steve had more than one father, and who at Ohio State didn't know Woody? Despite the explicit instructions, I'd yell down the hall, "Hey Steve, your dad is on the phone." In addition to being the head football coach, Woody also taught history. He despised smoking and enforced a strict no-smoking policy—students couldn't even bring cigarettes into the classroom but had to leave them outside. If Woody caught anyone breaking the rule, they were thrown out of class.

OSU was a college football powerhouse, and going to football games was a huge event. Back then, fifty dollars and a valid student ID granted a student entry to every Ohio State game in every sport except for basketball and hockey. Our IDs didn't include photos,

In front of an off-campus student apartment at Ohio State. My college grades weren't bad but would have been better if not for all those distractions available around campus. I had plenty of side hustles.

which presented an opportunity for another side hustle. On game days, for a small fee, we'd let someone else use our IDs to gain entrance to the game—*after* we did, of course. Once inside the stadium, we'd place our student IDs inside tennis balls (into which we had cut a small opening) and toss them to a waiting friend on the other side of the gate.

In my final year at school, the football team was undefeated, and on Jan 1, 1969, I made the trip to Pasadena, California, to watch OSU play in the Rose Bowl against the USC Trojans. O. J. Simpson made a spectacular 80-yard touchdown run in the second quarter, giving USC a 10-0 lead. After that incredible run, Woody told the team, "I don't care if we lose 50-0; that son of a bitch better not score another point." O. J. took a beating the rest of the game and never scored another point. The undefeated Buckeyes went on to win the game 27-16.

I knew Coach Hayes, and I was friends with many of the players, often spending time with them in the locker room during the regular season. I was sort of the unofficial team mascot. So after the game I found myself in the locker room with the team. While we were celebrating, O. J. walked in. He was already a major football star, having won the Heisman trophy that year. The room fell silent as we waited to see what would happen. O. J. broke the silence, saying, "You guys are the best damn team in the nation." The locker room erupted in chants, "O. J. . . . O. J. . . . O. J." It was an unforgettable day.

Getting By

My college grades weren't bad, but I was never at the top of my class. I had the brains, but there were too many distractions. Once, on my way to take a midterm exam, I was easily persuaded to skip the test and go skinny dipping with my buddy and some girls he knew. Often, once I had answered enough questions on a test to secure the grade I wanted, I'd turn in my paper and leave so I could move on to something else. This approach led to fluctuating grades, resulting in my academic probation seven times. Whenever I needed to boost my GPA, I took a phys ed class. I took enough of those that if I had taken just two more, I could have had a phys ed minor to complement my marketing major. While I don't dwell on regrets, I'll admit I should have put more effort into my schoolwork.

Back at home on break from school, I noticed how different my mother's side of the family was from my father's. Aunts and uncles on my mother's side would ask, "Are you having a good time? Are there lots of girls? Do you go to many parties?" On my father's side, they wanted to know if I brought my books home so I could study while I was home. I hadn't noticed that difference when I was younger.

For a marketing class project, I sent out business surveys about Bulova watches to twenty local jewelry stores. Cowell and Hubbard, Cleveland's oldest jewelry store at the time, was the only one to respond. Back home on summer break, I stopped by the store to thank the manager for responding to my survey and also to say hello to a neighbor who worked there. A tray of rings was left out on the counter, so I handed them to the manager for safekeeping. He asked if I was looking for a summer job. I already had a job as an electrician's helper, but I told him I could work part-time in the evenings. The store manager must've seen something in me that summer, because after I returned to school in the fall, he started sending me gifts every few months—first, a jeweler's eyepiece, then various other tools. I kept working at Cowell and Hubbard part-time during school breaks, utterly unaware that this was a step that would propel me into a lifelong career in the jewelry business—and, unexpectedly, into television.

No Rest for the Weary

I juggled several jobs while in college. From 11 a.m. to 2 p.m., I checked meal plan tickets in the cafeteria. From 4 p.m. to 6 p.m., I worked the phone switchboard. In the early evening, I'd do homework, hang out with friends or catch up on sleep. Then, from 11 p.m. to 7 a.m., I worked as a janitor in the dorm. The janitorial job was shared among the three of us, so I didn't work every night. With only three hours of class each day, I had plenty of time to study. I didn't get much sleep back then (and I still don't need much sleep now).

I worked as a waiter at a bar named North Heidelberg, although everyone called it The Northberg, located in the basement of an old building on High Street. The beer arrived in cases delivered to the lower-level bar via a chute. Empty bottles had to be carried back up in cardboard cases, so the beer truck could collect them the next day. Carrying the bottles up was a laborious task. After I'd been there a while, I often had some fun at the newcomers' expense. I would stack several beer cases and carry them up the stairs effortlessly. Bigger guys saw me tackling what seemed like a massive load, and not to be outdone by the little guy, they would carry two or three more cases than I did, which was no easy feat. What they didn't know was that my cases were empty. My biggest challenge was keeping the boxes from tipping over as I carried them up, since they were so light without the empty bottles.

One evening, the football team was at the bar and they started getting rowdy. I even heard one of the players talking about grabbing me and throwing me around like a football. Before things got out of hand, someone called Woody. The moment Woody walked in, the entire place went silent. Woody made a single motion with his thumb and shouted, "OUT!" The players walked out silently, like ducks in a row.

A Few Extra Bullets

I wanted to join the Reserve Officers Training Corps—ROTC, the leadership program that prepares college students for opportunities in the armed forces. When I went to the office to sign up, I was told that my height disqualified me from joining. This wasn't a surprise because in high school I had already been classified as 4-F, disqualified from service due to my height. But I never wanted to let my height get in the way. When I told the officer that I really wanted to join, he informed me that I would need to see Colonel Von Rohr. So I headed over to meet the colonel.

"What are *you* here for?" he asked, emphasizing *you* in an apparent reference to my height.

"I want to be in the ROTC."

"Why?"

"It's better than taking ten hours of math," I said. ROTC students were excused from taking some math courses.

"Okay, you're in," he said with a laugh.

I didn't have to wear a uniform or participate in mundane tasks like marching. After completing the two-year program, students could go on to earn the rank of second lieutenant. During the last class, they showed a film of a second lieutenant emerging from a foxhole, only to have his head blown off. The room went silent, and the sergeant, with all the gravitas he could muster, said, "Makes you wonder, doesn't it?" Not exactly a motivating way to kick off military training! I did not pursue the rank of second lieutenant, in case you were wondering.

You only hear "cease fire" on the firing range if something serious happens. Then, everyone stops firing, drops their weapon, and takes two steps back. With a long day of target practice dragging on, I was getting bored and decided to take a few shots at the target of the guy next to me. When he pulled in his target and saw more holes than should be there, he yelled "Cease fire!" That drew the immediate attention of the attending sergeant. The sergeant, immediately knowing it was me, barked, "Rinaldi, to my office. Now!" I was sure I was going to be kicked out. But when we got to his office, he looked at me and said, "Listen, no one likes a snitch." Then he added, "When it's time for the test, come see me." On test day, he handed me a few extra rounds and said with a wink, "Do what you need to do." Once again, I plunked a few extra holes in my neighbor's target. Mischievous should be my middle name!

The Graduate

At 9 a.m. on Mother's Day, I had just returned to the dorm from being out all Saturday night. As I was taking off my shoes, I heard a knock on the door. It was my father—unannounced. He explained that my mother wanted to attend at least one Mother's Day event at the school before I soon graduated. The event was just a meal in the cafeteria, but it seemed important to her. My father asked why I was up so early and already dressed. "I am getting ready for church," I told him with a straight face." He insisted I put on a suit, and although I was running on empty from being out all night, I obliged and off we went. I didn't know that my parents' visit had another purpose. Apparently, I had been invited to join the honor society, but I didn't know because the school had mailed the invitation to my home. We walked past the room where the ceremony was taking place, and my father insisted we go inside. To my shock, the speaker called my name a few minutes into the event. My grades weren't up to par, and I hadn't been involved with the organization at all, yet they had invited me to join anyway.

I had little interest in attending my college graduation ceremony, but my parents insisted. The day before the ceremony we had dinner together at a nice restaurant, but I was restless, and when my mother asked why, I explained that it was my last night at school, and I wanted to spend it with my friends. She understood, and after dinner we parted ways for the evening so I could have one final night out. As usual, I stayed out all night, and while I made it to graduation, I slept through most of the ceremony. A guy sitting behind me tapped me on the shoulder and said, "You don't know me, but we've had many classes together, and you slept through all of them. Can't you at least stay awake for graduation?"

"Shhh," I said. "I'm trying to sleep."

Before I could officially receive my diploma, I had a small matter of $200 in overdue parking fines to settle. Early on at college, I had bought a minibike that I used to ride around campus and to my various jobs. Everyone at school borrowed that bike, and together we racked up a mountain of tickets. Fortunately, my friends didn't stick me with the bill, and together, we collected enough money to pay the fines. When I left school, I sold the bike for fifty dollars—the same amount I paid for it.

On my first day at OSU, I had set a goal to know fifty people whenever I walked across the Oval. By graduation, I had become so well-connected that I knew nearly everyone who passed by.

BRIDGET THE MIDGET AND THE ALL-STARS

Now What?

With college in the rearview mirror, I considered the same questions most grads wonder about. What's next? Where will I live? What job will I have? Amid this uncertainty, I created a bucket list to help me focus on my goals. It included buying a house, taking a two-week vacation every year, and purchasing a shotgun—because I enjoyed hunting.

One of the summer jobs I held while in college was working for the State of Ohio on various light-duty construction projects. A man I knew from church got me the job. When I graduated and wasn't sure what I wanted to do, he offered me a full-time job with the state. I oversaw the relocation of families whose homes were being demolished to make way for highway construction.

I also relocated myself. After a brief stay with my parents, I moved into my own apartment. I also got my first car, my father's 1963 Comet. Up to this point in my life, I had relied mainly on others for rides. Even today, I'm not a big fan of driving, which I attribute to those early years of not being behind the wheel much.

Working for the state wasn't a bad job, but it wasn't something I saw myself doing long-term, so after about three years I left. I was also still working part-time at the jewelry store, so a full-time position in jewelry sales was a natural transition.

My parents had moved from my childhood home to Cleveland Heights, just a short drive from my job at Cowell & Hubbard. I was happy for them—and for me. I got to have dinner at their place every night, and Mom still did my laundry. Growing up with an Italian mother had its perks, especially for the guys in the family. Italian moms are famous for spoiling their sons. I don't recall ever seeing my mom sit down to eat. She was always fussing over us, making sure our napkins were perfectly placed and our plates were full, and she cleared dishes so the next course could be served.

"I've Got a Small Guy"

From 1963 to 1966, the city of Cleveland buzzed with excitement over a local television show: Ghoulardi's *Shock Theater*, which aired on WJW Channel 8. It was a strange show that got huge ratings. The host was Ernie Anderson, the station's announcer wearing a crazy wig, who showed old horror movies and made fun of them. His sidekick was Chuck "Big Chuck" Schodowski, a cameraman and production guy who was normally behind the scenes but who Ernie made part of the show. I had no idea how profoundly the show those two created would change my life in just a few short years.

Ghoulardi's *Shock Theater* show ended in 1966 while I was in college, when Ernie Anderson left Cleveland for Hollywood. Bob "Hoolihan" Wells, a weatherman, became co-host alongside Big Chuck. I was familiar with *The Hoolihan and Big Chuck Show*, but having been away at school in Columbus and then, after graduation, rarely home on Friday nights, I hadn't watched much of it. That was all about to change.

In the summer of 1971, I was working at Cowell and Hubbard when Dick Blake, a popular local entertainer and dance instructor, stopped in for a jewelry repair. While he waited, I made small talk with him.

Dick asked me, "Do you like making people laugh? You seem to enjoy being funny."

I told him I enjoyed talking with customers, and if I could get them to laugh and have a good time, that was even better.

"I know Hoolihan and Big Chuck; I could introduce you."

"Great, tell them to give me a call," I said. I gave Dick one of my cards, not for a moment thinking anything would come of it.

A few days later, the phone rang at the jewelry store.

"Cowell and Hubbard, how can I help you?"

"John Rinaldi? Big Chuck here. I got your name from Dick Blake. I think we can use you on the show."

At first, I thought, *Yeah, right, there's no way this is Big Chuck.* But after a few moments, I realized it was indeed Big Chuck, and he explained what he was looking for.

"I need someone short for a skit," Chuck said.

I would later learn that Chuck often called Dick when he needed an extra performer for the show, and this time he had called looking for a little girl. Dick told him, "I don't have a little girl, but I do know a little guy."

I told Chuck I would do it. He said he would mail me some things. A few days later, he called to ask about the mailing, but I hadn't received it.

"No problem," Chuck said. "We can work around that. Can you get a dress, a wig, and combat boots?"

"Sure," I replied. I would borrow the dress and wig from my sister, and a buddy just back from Vietnam had boots I could use.

"Great! We'll be filming at Bonnie's Lounge on West 260th and Lorain on Saturday. You know where that is?"

Bonnie's was on the West Side—a long drive from where I lived on the East Side, but I said I'd be there.

I made the trek across town along with three friends, and when we arrived at Bonnie's, the front door was locked. I knocked, and no one answered. At first I thought I'd driven all this way for nothing, but I don't give up that easily. I gave the door a strong thump, and this time Big Chuck opened it.

"Are you John Rinaldi?" he asked. How many other guys my height was he expecting to show up at the bar that night?

"I am. What's with the locked door?"

Chuck explained that since the station was paying for the beer, people already in the bar would be allowed to drink as much as they wanted but couldn't leave and return with more people.

I hadn't given much thought to what I'd be doing being in the skit, but when I stepped into that bar and realized I was about to be part of Cleveland's most popular TV show, the excitement kicked in.

Chuck introduced me to his wife and sister-in-law, who would be background dancers in the skit, and to the cameraman and the lighting guy. I introduced the friends who came with me.

It was a typical neighborhood bar. Chuck showed me where we would be filming, and I saw tables and chairs set up in front of where we would perform. This was where the audience for our act would sit. Chuck then briefed me on the shoot. He and I would lip-synch to the Ray Stevens song "Bridget the Midget (Queen of the Blues)." Chuck, dressed in a white suit, would start solo. Then I would run out, he would help me onto a table, and I would dance and lip-synch for the remainder of the song.

"We have to keep the shoot moving," Chuck warned me. "We only have a limited amount of time to film before the audience will lose interest."

"Don't worry about that," I said with youthful bravado.

Chuck directed me to a back room where the backup dancers had just finished with their costumes and makeup. I changed into the costume I had brought with me.

The skit was filmed in several takes: wide shots of me dancing and singing, close-ups of my feet, cutaways to the audience cheering us on, and footage of the background dancers. We filmed for

My first skit for *The Hoolihan and Big Chuck Show.* "I need someone short for a skit," Chuck told me over the phone. Check! Then he asked, "Can you get a dress, a wig, and combat boots?" And that was my start in television. *(Chuck Schodowski collection)*

about two hours. As I would come to learn well, for every minute of airable film, it took about an hour of actual shooting, including time to set up and move the camera for various shots.

Despite Chuck's warning, we never lost the audience. Between takes, I entertained by talking with people, flipping up my skirt, and otherwise goofing off—a skill I had already mastered pretty well.

Chuck was busy managing the production part of the shoot, but he also took time to talk with the audience, interacting with them as well as giving them direction.

I think Chuck was surprised that I was so comfortable performing in front of an audience. He didn't know that I had been entertaining people for years, giving speeches and often being the center of attention throughout school. Performing in a skit—even for television—wasn't intimidating to me; it was *fun*.

And that's how my television career started.

Don't Ask, I Might Say Yes

Based on my performance in the "Bridget the Midget" skit, that night, before we even left Bonnie's Lounge, Chuck asked if I wanted another assignment. "Would you like to join the Hoolihan and Big Chuck All-Star team?" I gladly accepted.

The All-Stars were a traveling sports team composed primarily of personalities from *The Hoolihan and Big Chuck Show*, plus some friends and family members, such as Chuck's brother Paul. The team played basketball, football, softball, and even hockey in the early days, but we eventually stopped playing hockey and football due to injuries. The games were played for charity, a tradition continued from the Ghoulardi show. The main roster included Big Chuck, Hoolihan, and me, along with a rotating lineup of players over the years, such as Big Stash, Herb "Soul Man" Thomas, Whoopee John, King Kong O'Kelly, Dr. G, Dave Stacey, Bernie Barabas, Ted Lux, Art Lofredo, Angel Rodriguez, Ron Ackerman, and Mark Elliott, the mayor of Brook Park.

At first we rode to games in a chauffeured bus, but that got too expensive and we eventually had to drive ourselves. This was before GPS, so finding some of those remote gyms felt like a scavenger hunt. Directions often include instructions like "turn right at the big red house" or "keep going until you see a road with no sign." And sometimes we were making these trips at night or in a winter snowstorm. It got to the point where we would drive into the main section of town and then have someone local, even the city police, escort us to the venue.

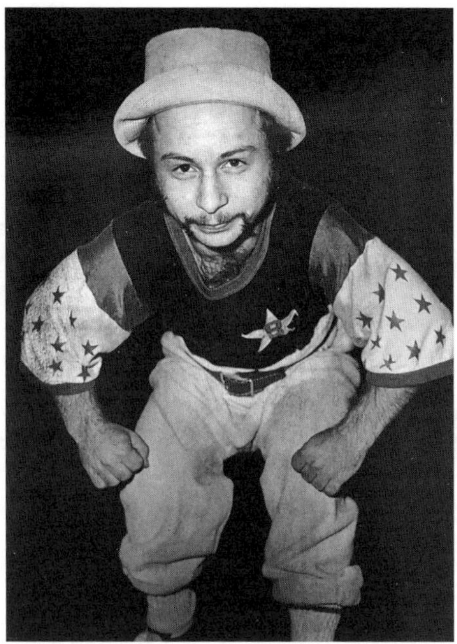

At my first appearance with the Hoolihan and Big Chuck All-Stars I didn't yet have either a nickname or a publicity photo. I soon got both. This is one of my first official publicity stills. *(Fox8)*

For my first basketball game, I showed up at the meeting spot for our bus in Brecksville. Hoolie and his wife were seated up front, but Russ, better known as "Big Stash," waved me to the back, where most of the guys hung out. There, things got a little more rambunctious. Most of the guys had a beer or two on the ride, and nature didn't take long to call. The only problem: No bathroom on the bus. So, the driver would ease into the right-hand lane, open the door, and two teammates would grab a guy by the belt while he leaned out to take care of business. Women rarely rode the bus, so our ridiculous antics stayed safely in the guy zone.

I brought a gym bag filled with sneakers, socks, shorts, and a shirt. Chuck gave me a team uniform shirt to wear. I put it on,

The All-Stars competed with local teams in softball and basketball, and we played for laughs. (We gave up football and hockey after too many injuries.) My uniform number was always 4; I was the shortest guy on the team, so I chose the number that was half of Channel 8.

and it hung like a dress down below my knees. No problem! That just added to the comedic effect.

Before each game, it was customary to announce the players as we ran out onto the basketball court to warm up. Because I was new to the team, the announcer didn't know how to introduce me, so I was introduced as "Bridget the Midget." Chuck brought a fright wig for me to wear.

Early in the game, while sitting on the bench, I overheard Hoolie ask Chuck, "What are we going to do with him?"

"Well, we have to put him in," Chuck said. "After all, I asked him to play, and he showed up. I can't let him sit on the bench the entire game." A short time later, Chuck gave me the nod to go in. Neither Chuck nor anyone else on the team knew that I had played competitive basketball in college on an intramural team, and despite my height, I was pretty good. (At the risk of bragging,

I was also the intermural doubles badminton champ and three-time tricycle race winner at Ohio State. I had a clear advantage in the tricycle races because unlike everyone else my knees weren't crammed into my chin while pedaling.)

I played well that night and earned a permanent spot on the All-Stars team. Chuck later told me he had only asked me to play out of courtesy and expected me to decline.

After the game, everyone signed autographs. Long lines formed for Bob and Chuck while the other players mingled with fans. I didn't have any publicity photos to sign, or a cool nickname yet, so I signed pictures of Hoolie and Chuck with "Bridget the Midget." A few lucky fans might still have one of those rare autographs.

Soon after that, Chuck coined my nickname—"Lil' John," a playful reference to my height and wordplay on Chuck's own nickname, "Big Chuck," given to him by Ernie Anderson.

Little did we know how fitting those nicknames would be for our show years later.

Code Red

During our All-Star games we performed special plays that we called "red plays"—comedic gags designed to entertain the crowd. During softball and basketball games, the umpire or referee would eject me from the game for one reason or another. The audience would boo. Chuck would plead for me to be allowed back, but I had my own revenge: I'd throw a shaving cream pie into the official's face. (We learned the hard way to use shaving cream instead of whipped cream—shaving cream wiped off easily, but whipped cream didn't, and turned into a sticky, smelly mess.)

We played more charity basketball games than any other sport because for those we didn't have to worry about the weather. We only took time off for Thanksgiving and Christmas.

Big Chuck, Dave Stacey, Del Vanichek, George Mondock, and me. Chuck's wife bought us all matching shirts. My hairline is struggling.

The games were played just for fun and to entertain the crowd. The entire team goofed off during the whole game. One of our classic red plays involved one of our players starting a fake fight with an opposing player. Then I'd announce, "There's only one way to settle this—like an old western, with a shoot-out!" Each "fighter" got a pistol and when our player fired, the entire opposing team would fall as if they had been shot. One of our players would grab the basketball and score while the "dead" team just lay there. (Of course, all these gags were preplanned, so everyone—including opposing players—knew what to do.)

For a while, Big Stash would carry me around on his shoulders. He was already tall, but with me perched on his shoulders, we looked like a giant—I could practically dunk the ball without even trying. Stash recently reminded me why we stopped this gag. One game, he tripped, and he managed to catch me just a couple of inches before I would have smashed face-first into the floor. After that, we decided the routine wasn't worth the risk.

During the breaks between quarters, Chuck and I would take over the basketball court with all sorts of antics. I might dress up in a tuxedo and lip-sync to Tom Jones songs while the cheerleaders joined me in evening gowns. One year, I dressed as Michael Jackson. Other times, Chuck and I would dress as clowns and perform in mime. We would meet midcourt and had a routine where our hats would fall off and my pants would fall down. It was all done in the slapstick style of vaudeville.

In an act we called "Physical Prowess," Chuck and I would do handstands off each other's backs. Almost every game featured me chasing the referee and throwing a bucket of water on him. I would follow that up by scaring the audience with the same bucket filled with confetti.

Our softball games featured a mix of skits and serious play. I played catcher, which made it easy to call out the red plays, and it was a perfect spot to banter with batters. I was mic'd for some games so the crowd could hear. One of our gags was using a grapefruit painted white to look like a softball. It would explode when a batter hit it. Sometimes I would tie a smoke bomb to the seat of my pants, or we'd stage a shoot-out on the pitcher's mound. Early on, Hoolihan pitched, and after he left, Whoopee John took over. Whoopee was a solid player in the Parma league. Chuck was our shortstop and stood out as an MVP. My buddy Joel, our tall first baseman, always rushed in to help me on close plays at the plate. Some runners came in hard, and we needed someone bigger to handle those slides; otherwise, they would've knocked me into next week.

When we played games against a team representing Catholic Charities for the Diocese of Cleveland, Bishop Anthony Pilla pitched. I always warned everyone, "Don't hit the Bishop." I thought that would be bad karma. We had good ballplayers who could hit the ball wherever they wanted, and I told them to hit anywhere but not up the middle. Whenever we managed to get the Bishop out, the nuns in the crowd would boo like we had committed a mortal sin.

A studio cameraman on our team would film parts of the games (it was actual film in the early days; later it was videotape), and the footage aired on the following week's Friday night show. Fans loved seeing themselves on TV, which helped draw a crowd to games. Unfortunately, the studio management decided that we could no longer film the games. I never understood that because it didn't cost the station anything—the cameraman was already with us.

The fun often continued after the games at a bar or some other event. One evening after an All-Star basketball game near Warrensville Heights, we went to an after-party at a local fire station. Tom Jones was performing nearby at Musicarnival, a popular summer tent theater that was a hot spot for live entertainment by nationally known acts. Well, we all liked music. Several of our basketball team members were musicians, and we frequently played impromptu concerts at our after-parties. Chuck played the banjo, I pretended to play along on my banjo, Mushmouth played the saxophone, and we had two accordion players: my good friend Dave and Whoopee John. Whoopee John was one of the original All-Stars after Chuck took over hosting the show, and he never missed a game. Well, this night we were in a rowdy mood so we decided to take our act to Musicarnival. With a line of people trailing behind Chuck and me, we walked across the street, marched into the event without a word from security, paraded through the audience, strolled across the stage right in front of Tom Jones, and exited through the back, all while playing "When the Saints Go Marching In." Tom Jones, clearly amused, announced to the crowd, "You guys paid to see that!"

BREAKS—LUCK AND NOT-SO-LUCKY

Not Dead Yet

In the summer of 1972, a drunk driver slammed head-on into my car. Although my friends riding in my car weren't seriously injured, I was driving and was pinned between my seat and the steering wheel. When the police arrived, they told my friends I was dead and to get away from the car. My friends quickly told them that I was conscious and talking. With the jaws of life, I was extracted from the vehicle and rushed to Charity Hospital.

When the doctor came in to examine me, he asked if I was "drunken." Between his heavy accent and my confusion from the blow to my face, I replied, "No, I'm Rinaldi." After I assured him that I wasn't drunk, he began examining me. Despite serious injuries that would have kept any rational person in the hospital, I signed myself out against the doctor's advice and I called my brother to pick me up. It was a rough night and I barely slept. I was in pain and extremely uncomfortable.

I had plans the next day to attend a football game with my father. With my car totaled, I called my father to let him know he would have to drive. I hadn't told him what happened. "You have that new car; why can't you drive?" he complained.

"I met a *smashing* salesman last night, and I'm getting a new car," I said.

When we got to the game, the pain had worsened from the

night before. Whenever fans stood to cheer, by the time I could get to my feet everyone else was already sitting back down. I managed to get through the game, and with my poor decision-making at its finest, I planned to attend a party later that evening. A friend picked me up, and he had the sound wisdom to take me right back home, knowing I should be in bed.

A few days later and still in pain, I stopped to see a doctor on the way back from picking up some jewelry. After a short examination, the doctor refused to let me leave and called an ambulance to take me to the hospital. I told the ambulance driver I wanted to go to Hillcrest Hospital. "This isn't a taxi service," he said. He told me he was taking me to the closest hospital.

If that accident happened today, I would probably be given a band-aid and be sent home the same day, along with a bill equivalent to several weeks' worth of paychecks. Instead, I was admitted to the hospital—and stayed for a month. In addition to a list of moderate injuries, my jaw was severely damaged, making it difficult to talk or eat. The doctors suggested re-breaking my jaw to reset it, but I refused. I told them I'd be fine as long as I could sip milkshakes and martinis through a straw while it healed. I lived in constant fear that every doctor entering my room was coming to break my jaw. Fortunately, I had a friend in the business—the renowned Cleveland neurosurgeon Dr. Robert White. He came to see me in the hospital, examined me, and reassured me that I would make a full recovery without having my jaw broken and reset.

To help me recover, weights were placed on my legs to stretch me out. I told the doctors to be careful with the weights because I wanted to leave at the same height I came in. The first few days were tough, but as time passed, my hospital stay felt more like a vacation. Hoolihan and Big Chuck announced on the air that I was in the hospital, which led to a flood of cards, gifts, and visitors. I had so many visitors that my bed had to be moved to the lounge area to accommodate the crowds. Every day, my buddy George brought a thermos of whiskey for me and took the empty one home. One night, the All-Stars showed up around 1 a.m. after a game, playing their instruments until security escorted them out. Eventually I was released, but I had to return every day for therapy. Despite the busted jaw and the pain, I had a surprisingly great month-long vacation.

I had hospitalization insurance through my job at Cowell & Hubbard. But I hadn't thought that coverage was sufficient, so I had purchased an additional personal health insurance policy. And, fortunately, it had taken effect the evening of the accident. I had made one payment on the policy, which activated it at 12:01 a.m. My car was hit approximately fifteen minutes later. The new coverage paid for everything. A Rinaldi life lesson: *Don't skimp on health insurance!*

One of my friends in the car that night was getting married, and the rest of us were either part of the wedding party or guests. I referred to the event as the "crippled crutch ceremony." The groom had his leg in a cast, another guy had his arm in a sling, and then there was me—still a mess weeks after the accident. To top it all off, the maid of honor had been in a boating accident and was recovering from a pretty serious injury. Despite being young and typically full of energy, by the end of the wedding reception we staggered out battered and bruised and ready for bed.

My Job as a Bouncer

In 1974, I began working weekends for Rene Cremona, a renowned local restaurateur, at his restaurant "Rene Cremona Presents." What was supposed to be a two-week gig for the grand opening turned into a two-and-a-half-year run. The restaurant was on Mayfield Road in Little Italy, on the East Side of Cleveland.

The three-level building housed three themed restaurants. The Baroque Turnip, a disco, was located in the basement. The Caprice Flamand, a fine Belgian restaurant, was on the ground floor. The top floor was a Roaring Twenties–style speakeasy called Joe Sent Me. I was the bouncer, doorman, and maître d' at Joe's. I wore a zoot suit and carried a gun in my vest, and patrons needed to tell me the password ("Joe sent me") before I would let them in.

The bar had a Prohibition-era vibe, with menus shaped like violins and drinks sneakily served in baby bottles and coffee mugs. The staff would stage several "raids" throughout the night to entertain the crowd. I'd be chased around the bar by other employees dressed as cops. Risqué pictures on the walls would spin around to reveal angelic paintings, and mannequins would transform into Salvation Army workers.

One of the regular music acts at the club was Tons of Fun, a trio of talented ladies that included Carmella Giampaolo. I convinced them to let me join their act. During the chorus of "Me and My Shadow," the girls would flip their skirts up, and I'd spring out, much to the crowd's delight. I told Big Chuck about Carmella, and she soon became a regular on *Hoolihan and Big Chuck*, often played my wife in skits. Tony Carmen, who was already a regular cast member of the show, also performed at Joe's with his band, the Tony Carmen Trio. On the TV show, he was best known for his role as "Kishka," the sidekick to Chuck's "Kielbasy Kid" character—like the Lone Ranger and Tonto.

One Sunday, after a Browns game, Rene called and asked me to come in and wait tables. I had never waited tables before, but he said he needed all the help he could get. My performance as a waiter fell far below even my own low expectations. The place was busy, and I wasn't used to the chaos. Instead of placing food directly in front of the customers as any experienced waiter would, I stood at the end of the table and asked everyone to pass the dishes down. And that was one of my better moments. A generous table left me a fifty-dollar tip, but as the guy left, he stopped me and said, "I'd like to give you another tip: Find another job."

I wasn't cut out to be a waiter, and was glad to return to my regular post at the door. That's where I learned another important lesson. To accommodate one regular customer, I needed to move a table to another spot in the bar. Having seen servers easily move tables, I attempted to place this high top between two other tables. As I was getting the table into position, I accidentally hit a woman in the head—and knocked her out cold. The crowd thought it was part of the act, and the band kept playing. When the woman regained consciousness, I apologized profusely. Thankfully, it was a time when people weren't so litigious, and she accepted my apology. Her party ate and drank for free that night!

One of the best parts of working for Rene was getting to work with my father. When Rene needed someone to host and liven up the downstairs club, I recommended my dad. At sixty-six, he was an instant hit.

Rene eventually left Cleveland, and I moved across the street to a small restaurant called The Tipsy Grape. It was a wine-and-cheese joint and a hot spot for pre- or post-show visits to Severance Hall. I was hired as a sommelier and worked for tips. The owner told me that if a customer ordered wine they didn't like, I should taste it, and if it tasted like Alka-Seltzer and vinegar, it was bad; otherwise, tell them that the wine wasn't bad but they may have made a poor selection, and we'd be glad to exchange it. Most people kept the wine. At the end of each week, John would give me a bottle of wine to try, and he would tell me all about it. He'd explain about tannins, acidity, body, and flavor. I drank enough wine to intoxicate the entire population of Cleveland, but to this day, all I know is what I like and don't like.

Hoolihan and Big Chuck . . . and Me

My role on *The Hoolihan and Big Chuck Show* changed over time. I started as a bit player, cast solely for my height in the "Bridget the Midget" skit, and I might have remained pigeonholed in those types of roles if it weren't for Hoolihan taking on more freelance work out of town. With his co-host often unavailable, Chuck began leaning on me more for skits. It didn't take long before he realized I could play virtually any character—a businessman, a crook, a guy on the street—regardless of size. Hoolihan's absence had another benefit for me: I began filling in for him on personal appearances with Chuck and the rest of the cast.

I had also now been playing regularly with the Hoolihan and Big Chuck All-Stars team for several years. Before games, the All-Stars team members were typically announced in increasing order of their popularity and importance to the show, starting with cast family members and new team players, eventually building to Hoolihan and Big Chuck. When I joined team, I would be one of the very first players announced. Over the years, however, my status gradually progressed until I was being introduced right before Hoolihan and Big Chuck. My spot in the lineup was a clear sign to me that Chuck felt my value to the show was growing. From bit player I had become a core part of the team and the show.

I never saw myself as a celebrity—then or later—but it didn't take long before the public began to see me differently. I was being recognized everywhere I went. Unlike most of the other regular cast members, who did their jobs inside the TV8 building, I was out in the public every day and accessible. At the jewelry store, anyone could see me at any time, and customers often gave me a shout as soon as they walked in: "Hey, Lil' John!" When I walked out on the busy downtown streets during the workday, people began stopping to talk or take a picture if they had a camera with them.

It was no different when Sherry and I went out in the evening. Even when I was driving, people would pull up next to me at a light to wave and yell hello if our windows were down. This was all brand-new to me, and I loved every minute of it.

At the TV station, I had built strong relationships with most of the staff and on-air talent. When it comes to relationships, I've always said I'm like Switzerland—neutral. I want to get along with everyone. Even early on, I found I clicked with almost everybody. Turns out it wasn't just my charming personality. I noticed a fair amount of competition among some employees, particularly among the on-air talent. Employees were often jockeying for a different job they coveted; for example, a newscaster on the late-night slot might be angling for a spot on the more prestigious six o'clock news. I'm not implying that people didn't like each other or get along, but there was often an underlying level of competitive tension in the air. But everyone at the station knew I already had a full-time career in the jewelry business. I wasn't looking to take anyone's spot at the station, so I wasn't a threat. As a result, I had a much more relaxed friendship with people there.

In the early days, I wasn't in the TV studio very often, but when I was, I always had to be buzzed in the door and escorted wherever I needed to go. But as my popularity grew and the staff got to know me, that changed. Eventually, I was issued my own employee pass, giving me the freedom to enter the building whenever I needed.

I wasn't the only bit player rising through the ranks. In 1973, while taking night classes in TV production, Art Lofredo sent Chuck a skit idea that he wound up using on-air. Soon after, TV8 hired Art for station production duties. Chuck began casting Art in skits, and used him more frequently whenever Hoolihan's out-of-town schedule left a gap. Art became a fan favorite early on, starring in now-classic skits like "The Streak" and "The Junk Food Junkie."

While the exact date escapes me, it was around 1976 when my status as a core cast member was officially recognized. Chuck aired a special show dedicated entirely to me: "Lil' John Night." Every skit that night featured me. I had come along way from those early days of being cast solely for my height.

While I had become more of an insider, there was still a separation between the other cast members and me. I spent little time at the station because most of our skits were shot on location, and our personal appearances and All-Stars ballgames took place far from the station. Most of the others worked at TV8 and spent a great deal of time together there. Chuck was a producer and director for several shows, Art Lofredo was part of the production team, and Hoolihan was a fixture on the air as the weatherman. Even Herb "Soul Man" Thomas worked at the station in various roles before eventually becoming a camera operator.

So as much fun as I was having with the show, for me it was still just a side gig. It wasn't something I spent much time thinking about outside of shooting skits or making personal appearances. I was enjoying the ride, never suspecting that it would lead to something much bigger.

SHE DIDN'T SAY NO

Gotta Find a Woman

My friend Dave invited me to see his band at the Last Stop Inn in Parma. I arrived around 10 p.m., coming straight from work at the jewelry store. Still in my suit and tie, I joined a crowd of regulars there to see the band. One of them was Sherry, a beautiful girl whose brother-in-law was the band's drummer. It was her birthday, so I bought her a drink, and we danced a few songs. A few weeks later, right before Valentine's Day, I was at another gig with Dave's band, and so was Sherry. At one point during the evening, Dave said, "Don't forget, John, we have a double date tomorrow, and the girl's dad won't let her go out with me unless it's a double."

"Sorry, Dave, I completely forgot. I don't have a date." I turned to Sherry and said, "What are you doing tomorrow night?"

"I'm baking cookies for my parents' twenty-fifth anniversary party."

"How about going out with me instead?"

Sherry remembers it a little differently. The way she tells it, I, with all the bravado of an obnoxious used car salesman, leaned in and said, "Listen, I sell things for a living and I am going to convince you to go out with me tomorrow night."

Either way, Sherry didn't agree right away, so I kept up the playful banter. Finally, her sister cut in. "Oh, for the love of God, Sherry, just go out with him. I can't listen to him beg anymore."

Our first few dates were always in groups—my usual strategy

It took a little convincing to get Sherry to go out on a date with me the first time, but I was a pretty good salesman. Here we're having a great time in Niagara Falls in 1974.

back then. We didn't go out alone until our fourth date, when we had dinner at the Marriott Hotel on West 150th Street near the airport. Before you get any ideas, this was the early '70s, when hotel restaurants were considered among the best in town. As we talked, I browsed the menu with one eye while the other remained focused on Sherry. We ordered our dinners, and the waiter returned a few minutes later. He started mixing spices, eggs, and a lovely cut of meat right at the table. I watched in fascination, thinking, "Wow, this will be great!" After a minute or two, he carefully placed the mixture on my plate. He then stood there, staring at me with a look that said, *go ahead, try it*. After an uncomfortably long silence, I said, "That's funny, pal—why don't you take it in the back and cook it now?" It turns out I had missed the word "raw" in the description of steak tartare. I took a bite, and while I did enjoy it, I wound up taking most of it home and I cooked it the next day—the way I thought it should have been prepared the first time.

I didn't usually introduce anyone I was dating to my parents, but after Sherry and I had been dating a while and it became serious enough, it was time. Before we arrived at my parents house for dinner, I gave her one piece of advice: "When my father asks—and he will—if you're Italian, just say yes." Sherry did have some Italian heritage, so it wasn't a complete fib. Dinner was going smoothly, but, as we finished our meals, my mother cheerfully announced, "It's time for cannoli!"

Brimming with enthusiasm, Sherry asked, "What's a cannoli?"

Busted!

After seeing how my mom fussed over the men at the dinner table, Sherry later told her mom, "If he thinks I'm going to wait on him like that, he's crazy." She set me straight the first time we had dinner at her place. "John, the food isn't going to jump onto your plate; you have to use the spoon and put it there." Message received!

Romance? How About a Ring Instead?

It was 1974. I had been appearing in skits on *The Hoolihan and Big Chuck Show* and playing with the All-Stars for three years, was working at Rene Cremona's, and my jewelry sales career was thriving. Life was going well—and it was about to get better.

One evening, while watching *Hoolihan and Big Chuck* with Sherry, one of my skits came on. Usually, when one of my bits aired, Sherry and I would stop talking to watch. But this time, mid-sketch, I casually asked, "Do you think we'll ever get married?"

"Yeah, I think so," she said matter-of-factly,

I reached into my pocket and pulled out a ring.

"Okay, here's your engagement ring."

No buildup, no roses, no moonlit stroll—just me, the TV glowing in the background, and that now famous laugh from the show. Sherry and I hadn't talked about marriage at all before, so this was a total surprise to her.

She was thrilled—at first. Over the years, though, she has often pointed out that it was the least romantic proposal ever. Whenever she brings that up, I always reply, "You didn't say no!"

Given my work in the jewelry business, I'd heard all kinds of romantic stories—from rose petals leading to a heart-shaped ring box to extravagant weekend getaways with hot-air balloons. And here I was, handing my future wife her engagement ring like I was passing her another slice of pizza. Sherry, I promise I'll do better if we ever get engaged again.

Sherry and I went to confession before we got married. My friends joked that I was probably in the confessional booth so long that they had to change the lightbulb. (A lightbulb indicates when someone is in the confessional. It's like the " no vacancy" sign at a motel.) Years later, during the Year of Forgiveness, Sherry and I went to confession again. We figured we should check in, considering it had been forty-five years since our last confessions. I remembered going to confession when I was little with simple sins: "Father, please forgive me, I lied to my parents." This time, I told the priest, "Father, it's been a long time since my last confession; you'd better give me one of everything except murder." The priest didn't flinch. Perhaps he was accustomed to people like me attempting to make a quick spiritual escape. My penance was one Our Father and one Hail Mary, the equivalent of a "Get Out of Jail Free" Catholic monopoly card. On the other hand, Sherry—a saint compared to me—was asked to write a letter to the church confessing her sins.

Sherry and I were married at St. John's Cathedral in downtown Cleveland in May 1975. It was a grand day, made even more special

My proposal wasn't the most romantic, but it worked! And don't knock my powder-blue tux and ruffled shirt—it was the Seventies! (Fashion courtesy of American Commodore Tuxedo, in exchange for an on-air plug.)

by being chauffeured in my friend's beautifully restored 1936 Rolls-Royce. Sherry wore a conservative but elegant white gown. I wore a powder-blue tuxedo. No wisecracks! It was fashionable then. At the time, I was doing Tom Jones impersonations for the TV show, and American Commodore Tuxedo supplied me with free tuxedos for the show and also for my wedding in exchange for an on-air plug.

The ceremony was about to start, but my groomsmen were nowhere to be found. After searching for several minutes, I found them outside on the street corner. They thought the best way to prepare for my big moment was chowing down on hot dogs from the street vendor.

After the ceremony, we invited the bridal party back to our house to hang out until the reception. We did this partly because we were worried the groomsmen would start drinking and not return for the reception. It was held at the Celebrity Room in Mayfield Heights. Their menu of forty-two dessert selections sold me on the place. After our reception, Sherry and I and the bridal party went across the street to a well-known bar called Saints and Sinners in the Eastgate Plaza to continue the party. We didn't get home until 4:30 a.m., shortly before we were scheduled to leave for our honeymoon.

Honeymoon Hiccups

Our honeymoon lasted two weeks and was the longest vacation Sherry and I would have for many years. After we got married, I could only manage a day off here and there or the occasional long weekend. It wasn't until I opened my own store in 1980 that we could take another extended vacation.

We began our honeymoon with a trip to Disney and Fort Lauderdale, but we got off to a bumpy start. After landing at the airport, we took a cab from the terminal to the rental car company, and the cab driver was grumbling about how short the trip was. Upon arrival, I paid the fare and doubled the amount for a tip. The driver looked at me and asked, "Is that all you're going to give for a tip?"

I'm a generous tipper and I thought doubling the amount was appropriate, but he kept complaining. We were anxious to get moving, but the driver kept delaying getting our luggage from the trunk. I finally had enough and said, "You're right—that tip isn't right." I reached out, took back the entire tip, and said, "Now you get nothing."

At that point, he went into a rage. He stormed out of the car and began throwing our luggage into the street. Alarmed, Sherry asked what we should do. "Grab your luggage and run!" Running has always been my response to signs of danger.

Fort Lauderdale was home to the New York Yankees' spring training facility. When I worked at Rene Cremona's, Al Rosen, the general manager for the Indians, used to come in regularly. Al was in Fort Lauderdale and stayed at the same hotel as Sherry and me. When he saw me, he invited us to a party in George Steinbrenner's private suite. George's bathroom was twice the size of our entire hotel room, and I kept trying to see the rack room rate, which was posted on the back of the front door.

A couple of nights later, we went to see a comedian perform. Sherry and I like to sit at the bar so we can interact with other people. We grabbed two seats, and it wasn't until after we sat down that I realized the guy sitting next to me was Mickey Mantle. I discreetly leaned over to my wife and, while trying to contain my excitement, whispered, "Mickey Mantle is sitting next to me." Sherry whispered back with the same enthusiasm, "Who is Mickey Mantle?" I asked for an autograph, but in the chaos of drinks and the late hour, I accidentally left it behind at the bar. The lesson? Don't drink and autograph!

The final part of our honeymoon was a weeklong cruise. Cruises were a fancy affair back then and guests were expected to dress for dinner. Sherry and I had suitcases so big that I could fit inside them, and they were packed to the brim. Among my belongings were two tuxedos—one lime green and one yellow, a burnt orange sports coat, and five suits. I know what you're thinking, and yep, I am still a snappy dresser today!

After boarding the cruise ship and settling in, we went to register for dinner. Three couples ahead of us didn't seem thrilled with any of the accommodations, complaining about the times and seating arrangements. When it was our turn, the poor guy handling the registrations looked utterly drained. He asked if we preferred early or late seating, and I casually said, "Late is fine." Then, he asked if we had any seating preferences. I shrugged and said, "No, as long as we get the same food as everyone else, it doesn't matter." Surprised and relieved at how easy we were making this process, he smiled and gave us our seating assignments. When we arrived at dinner, we were shocked to learn we were seated at the captain's table—the best seats in the house! It pays to be nice.

We immediately hit it off with two young ladies seated at our table, and also the waitstaff. Our Caribbean cruise visited St. John, St. Thomas, and St. Martin. When we left the ship to tour the islands, we went with our new friends. When the ship was ready to leave the dock, it would signal with a single horn blast ten minutes before departure: Time for passengers to return. Two blasts signified that the ship was pulling away. While out exploring, we had lost track of the time when suddenly we heard that first blast. The waiter and busboy bolted, leaving the rest of us struggling to keep up. We heard the second blast of two horns just as we arrived back at the port, with barely enough time to jump on board as the ship began to pull away.

It might seem odd that we became friends with the crew, but honestly, I've never been one to judge people by their job titles or social status. I don't care where someone's from or what they do for a living; as long as people are friendly and want to have a good time, that's all that matters to me.

Sherry and I decided to throw a little party in our room for our new friends, but there was one small problem—food. We couldn't order delivery, so we had to improvise. During the all-you-can-eat dinner, I came prepared with a shopping bag discreetly tucked between my legs. It happened to be lobster night, and every time a lobster landed in front of me, I quietly slipped it into the bag. By the end of dinner, I had a solid stash of lobsters for the party. The guys managed to get a whole cheese wheel, and the girls brought an assortment of appetizers.

On the final night of the cruise, an awards ceremony was held, and guests received accolades for achievements such as Best Basketball Player and Best Dressed. Sherry and I were thrilled to

With my lovely bride on our honeymoon. (And another American Commodore Tuxedo outfit.) We started at the captain's table but wound up hanging out with the crew—and nearly got left behind at one port.

win the award for Best Honeymoon Couple. But I had another surprise waiting for me. A couple of categories later, the announcer declared, "John Rinaldi wins for Best Single Passenger!" Sherry liked to go to bed early, and still does, and I enjoy staying up late. So after she turned in for the night, I'd head over to the bar for drinks. Later in the evening the bar was mostly filled with singles, so I was assumed to be single. When the presenter handed me the award, he looked utterly baffled and said, "You're married? You were at the bar every night!" Whenever I tell this story, people ask Sherry, "Weren't you upset?" She laughs. "No! What's he supposed to do—watch me sleep?"

Getting off the ship, we ran into luggage issues again. The customs agent told me I had to put the luggage on the table. The table was almost as tall as I was and our bags were heavy. I said I couldn't lift them that high and asked for assistance. He told me they weren't allowed to help. I suggested leaving the cases on the ground and examining them there. Meanwhile, two hundred people are waiting behind us, and everyone is getting annoyed. The agents finally rummaged through our luggage, on the floor, like we were international smugglers, and left our belongings a complete mess.

Luggage issues seem to follow us everywhere. Years later, on our way back from a trip to Italy, Sherry and I were going through baggage checks at the airport when I noticed oil all over the conveyor belt, dripping onto the floor. I turned to Sherry and said, "Look at this—some idiot spilled oil everywhere!" After we got through security, I reached for my jacket and discovered it was soaked in oil. "That idiot got oil all over my jacket!" I complained. Then, I grabbed my carry-on, and oil started seeping out of that as well. That's when it hit me—one of the bottles of olive oil we bought on our trip had busted. That idiot was me!

Sherry and I cook a lot with olive oil—so much that we usually buy it by the gallon. We had toured an olive oil factory on our trip and picked up a few bottles since the company didn't export to the U.S.

With my suitcase ruined, I rushed to a nearby store to replace it, but they didn't sell luggage. What they did have were heavy-duty garbage bags. I emptied my oil-soaked suitcase and stuffed all my belongings into the bags. Then I dragged my clothes around the airport in garbage bags like a hobo.

Mysterious Mr. P

Once, on our way back from a sales trip to Hawaii that I won while working at Cowell & Hubbard (yes, I'm still bragging about it), we decided to stop for a few days in Las Vegas. No surprise, the adventure started with the airline losing our luggage. I couldn't just buy new clothes because all my clothes had to be altered. We spent three days in Vegas hand-washing our clothes in the sink, which was as glamorous as it sounds.

The first morning, I went down to the craps table to kill some time while Sherry was still getting ready. Armed with knowledge I'd gained from reading a book on winning at craps, I was convinced I was about to clean up. I was placing modest bets of a dollar or two at the end of the table when a guy at the other end called out.

"You'll never win big betting like that."

"This is all I've got," I said.

He had racks of hundred-dollar chips in front of him, and he tossed twenty-five-dollar chips to the staff like they were spare change. The staff catered to his every need, and everyone called him "Mr. P." "Do you need another drink, Mr. P?" "Can I get you anything else, Mr. P?"

"That's it, I gotta go," Mr. P announced abruptly. He vanished from the table in a flash, leaving his chips behind. Within seconds, the staff collected and counted his winnings. A few minutes later, Sherry came down, and before I could recount the strange interaction, a gentleman in a tuxedo approached. He asked if I was the guy playing craps with Mr. P, and I said yes. He said Mr. P had instructed him to "take care" of me. He then asked what we wanted to do in town. I mentioned a show I wanted to see. "When you get to the venue," he said, "just walk up to the door and go right in. Everything will be taken care of."

When Sherry and I arrived at the show that night, the line was a mile long. "Let's just go to the door, like the guy said," I told Sherry. She was nervous that we'd be turned away, so I told her to stay put and I'd check it out. When I got to the door, I noticed a board with names written in black, and mine was in red. The doorman asked for my name, and when I gave it he said, "Come right in, Mr. Rinaldi." I ran back to get Sherry, and she warned me that I had better not be lying. We were escorted to the best private booth in the house. It was the kind of place where they bring two drinks when you order one, but when I ordered, they only brought one. I asked about the second drink. "We don't want the ice to melt in your drink, Mr. Rinaldi," the waiter replied. When the bill came, it said, "Complimentary. Do not pay." I did some mental math to figure out an appropriate tip and left it on the table. I had been tipping appropriately and generously to the maître d' and the wait staff the entire evening. As we left, the maître d' stopped me and asked if we enjoyed the show. I told him it was great. He shook my hand and returned all the tip money I had left for every employee. When I protested, he said, "No, Mr. Rinaldi, everything has been taken care of."

The next day at the hotel, Mr. P's tuxedo-wearing concierge appeared again out of thin air, like some casino fairy godfather. He asked how we enjoyed the show and what we wanted to do that evening. For the rest of our stay, we were treated like high rollers—eating, drinking, and being entertained for free. When Sherry and I were checking out of the hotel, we discovered that Mr. P had not only taken care of our entertainment but also our hotel room. To this day, I still have no idea who Mr. P was, but he sure made our trip unforgettable.

As we stepped outside to get into the cab taking us to the airport, our lost luggage was being delivered—in that very same cab.

Speechless in Vegas

On a solo trip to Vegas with my buddies, we were seated at a table front and center for a Paul Anka show. On the other side of our table sat a large man with an attractive young woman, and right behind him stood a man who appeared to be his bodyguard. The man was talking non-stop through the show—a real blowhard. I noticed the woman had a black-and-blue mark on her arm, and I realized it was from him repeatedly tapping her on the same spot to get her attention. At one point, the guy offered me a drink from his bottle. I said, "Sure," and poured myself a glass and filled one for each of my three friends. He looked at me, chuckled, and said, "Hey, you've got a lot of balls, buddy. I offered you a drink, not your whole crew."

Paul Anka came to the edge of the stage and started singing directly to the pretty girl. The big guy waved him off, "Hey, go sing to someone else, pal." Toward the end of the show, the big guy stood up and announced, "I don't need any more of this shit. I don't like this guy anyway," and walked out. Two minutes later, he came back. Then, unexpectedly, he looked across the table at me and said, "That's a pretty girl. You like her?"

I was unsure where this was going, so I replied, "Yeah, she's pretty."

"Well, if you like her, you can have her," he said, casually.

It was one of the few times in my life when I was speechless. Not knowing what else to say or do, I excused myself and went to the bathroom. My buddies eventually came looking for me and said, "Hey, the big guy's asking where you went." I wasn't about to go back out there to find out what this was all about, but whatever it was, I wasn't interested. I didn't want to end up buried in the desert.

From Picnic to Panic

Sometime in the mid-1980s, Sherry and I went on a long weekend getaway to Kane, Pennsylvania—a small town in the middle of nowhere, on the edge of the Allegheny National Forest. We stayed at Kane Manor, a historic bed and breakfast located in a heavily wooded area. We thought a picnic lunch in the forest would be perfect on Saturday afternoon. I had a blanket in the car, so we grabbed a pizza and a bottle of wine to enjoy on one of the "easy-to-follow" wooded trails. There were trails of different lengths—one mile, two miles, and so on—but they all looped back to the hotel. Each was marked with a different color painted on trees. We picked a path and off we went. We found a nice spot and settled in with our pizza and wine. After eating, we packed up and headed back to the manor, taking with us the empty wine bottle and a pizza box with half the pizza left.

We walked along, paying little attention to anything except the colored trail markings on the trees, until suddenly we entered a clearing where every tree in sight had been tagged with different colored paint marks. Some pranksters must have deliberately set out to confuse hikers, and it was now impossible to tell which markings were the real trail.

At this point, every direction looked the same. We picked what looked like the right path to get back, but the tree markings eventually disappeared, leaving us deep in the woods with no clue where to go. That's when Sherry and I remembered a story the hotel manager had told us the night before about a couple who supposedly got lost in the forest and were eaten by bears. We had laughed it off as a joke, but it wasn't so funny now. After wandering for a couple of hours we were still in the middle of nowhere.

"Maybe we should leave the pizza, John." Sherry said. "The bears can smell it, and they might come after us."

"Bears don't like pizza," I said.

"What do you mean they don't like pizza? How do you know?"

"You ever see a bear ordering take-out pizza?" I was trying to keep things light.

Eventually, we stumbled on a small, old shelter. "Look, worst-case scenario, we could stay here for the night," I said.

"John!" Sherry shot back. "We're not spending the night out here to get eaten by bears." At this point, I could tell Sherry had had enough and was starting to panic. She threw the remaining pizza into the woods—but held onto the box (can't be littering, after all). "We didn't tell anyone we were leaving for the weekend, and no one from the hotel even knows we are in the woods."

I tried to calm her. "Don't worry. When we don't check out tomorrow evening as planned, they'll come looking for us." That didn't help.

We kept wandering for another hour, and as I began getting nervous myself, by some miracle, we stumbled out of the woods—right behind the bed and breakfast. It had been six hours since we left, and if you ask Sherry, she'll say we barely survived. To this day, Sherry won't even go to the Metroparks with me.

My Wonder Woman

Sherry and I raised two fantastic boys, Johnny and Dino. Let me rephrase—*Sherry* raised two wonderful boys. Between running the jewelry store, juggling my responsibilities for the show, and making personal appearances, I wasn't home nearly as much as I would have liked or probably should have been. Sherry, meanwhile, was a one-woman powerhouse. She packed lunches, provided taxi services for the kids to endless activities, and kept our house running like a finely tuned watch.

Despite missing many family events because of my work schedule, I always did what I could to contribute. For instance, at Christmas I made sure the house was beautifully decorated so everyone could enjoy the holiday. I often got home late, after everyone was in bed. Despite the hour, I'd drag out the ladder and head outside to hang Christmas lights. I'd be up on the roof or dangling off the ladder and I often thought that if I were to slip and fall into the bushes, no one would find me until the morning after I had frozen to death! Clark Griswold from the movie *Christmas Vacation* had nothing on me when it came to holiday light decorating.

A neighbor kid, trying to be funny, would yank on the ends of the lights I'd just hung up, and pull them down. The next evening I'd string them back up again. This little game lasted several nights until I finally figured out who it was and had a chat with his parents. Years later, I learned that the kid, now an adult, had purchased our old house in Brook Park, the one we owned before moving to Solon. One evening, Sherry and I drove by our old digs, and I saw him hanging up Christmas lights. I was tempted to return later and pull a few down, but my good-hearted wife wouldn't let me.

At Halloween, I always enjoyed taking the kids trick-or-treating. One year, I got a clown costume for myself, complete with a mask; it was a child's size, of course. John was still pretty young, so I thought I'd show him how to fill up his bag quickly. We hit the first house, and when the lady dropped candy into my bag, I asked, "Can I have some extra candy for my sick brother?" Because of my size, no one realized I was an adult in disguise. As we walked away, I told John, "That's how it's done, kid."

One of our next stops was at the house of a neighbor who was a lovely lady, but a bit high-strung. Instead of opening the door for trick-or-treaters, she would reach through the screen door, part of which she had removed, to hand out candy. I thought it would be funny to give her a trick. When she dropped the candy into my bag, I grabbed her arm and began demanding, in a crazy, agitated way, "More candy! Give me more!"

She started yelling for her husband. "Come quick! The clown's got me!" I wanted to give her a scare, not a heart attack, so quickly I pulled off my mask. "You son of a bitch!" she said, laughing. "I should take all that candy back."

It wasn't unusual for my kids to see their dad dressed in funny costumes, or covered in paint, or rummaging through mom's closet looking for a dress to wear. They'd grown up with me always doing something a little weird. It was usually because of the show, but actually they never connected the dots between their dad's bizarre actions and my role as a popular TV figure—even though they both had Big Chuck's picture hanging on their bedroom walls. I was just dad to them.

Home Sweet Hotel

When Sherry and I were first married, we lived in a little house in Brook Park. Later, we decided to move to Solon. We didn't expect the Brook Park house to sell so quickly and our new house wasn't ready yet. We asked the soon-to-be owners if we could rent our old place from them until our new home was finished. They agreed, but with one unusual condition: I had to autograph the hallway wall.

We would be moving shortly after the new school year began, so we enrolled our kids in the Solon school system. Sherry drove them back and forth from Brook Park every day. The school discovered that we weren't living in Solon yet and informed us that we would have to pay a substantial amount to continue attending. I explained that our new house was scheduled to be finished in about three weeks, but the school district was not budging. Rather than pay the exorbitant fee, I came up with a less costly plan: For the final three weeks of construction, we moved into a hotel in Solon. The school now had to send a bus to pick up and drop off the kids at the hotel. The kids loved the novelty, but Sherry and I found it a major hassle—especially when it came to eating out and finding entertainment. More than a few nights we wandered around the local department store to pass the time. One afternoon, when the kids were at school, Sherry and I were heading back to our hotel room when a guy staying a few rooms down recognized me and noticed the beautiful young woman I was with. Misunderstanding the situation, he yelled, "Hey, Lil' John! Good for you! *Go, go, go!*"

"No—this is my wife!" I yelled back.

Getting to Know You

Sherry and I celebrated our fiftieth wedding anniversary in 2025. Fifty years of love and laughter, but that also means we've survived all the phases of marriage: the honeymoon, raising kids, and the empty nest. Over the years, we've learned all the little things that make a spouse your spouse. Like when there are just five minutes left in the movie, and one person announces, "I'm tired; I'm going to bed," while the other person, in disbelief, protests, "How can you go to bed right when we're about to find out who did it?" (The response is, "When I'm tired, I'm tired. What can I say?")

Sherry and I have gotten many things right in our marriage, but there are a few things we still struggle with. One is putting up the Christmas tree together. Every year, like clockwork, we argue. Perhaps we can resolve that over the next fifty years. We also can't agree on who controls the thermostat. I like it warmer, but Sherry prefers a temperature suitable for storing meat. So I put on a sweatshirt. You don't stay married for fifty years by turning every little difference into a war. We've figured out how to laugh together, even when things go wrong. It also helps to learn how to say "I'm sorry" without actually admitting any wrongdoing.

Sherry, here's to fifty years of shared memories and building a wonderful family and life together. While the next fifty years might involve more naps and less dancing, I'm hopeful they'll be as wonderful as the first.

GETTING INTO BUSINESS

Brother, Can You Spare Several Thousand?

When I began working at Cowell & Hubbard Jewelers, it felt like family. Management would call us during the holidays to thank us for our hard work and encourage us to spend time with our families. But by the late 1970s, things had changed. Instead of appreciation for the twelve-hour workdays and encouragement to enjoy well-deserved time off at holidays, we got calls from the bean counters insisting we stay at work until our sheets were balanced.

I decided it was time to open my own jewelry store. I had been kicking around the idea for a little while, but now I was ready to get moving on it.

To start my own business, I needed a loan. I visited several banks, and my loan request was rejected at every one. It was the age-old story of the chicken or the egg: "We can't lend you money; you don't have enough equity." Well, if I had enough equity, I wouldn't need you!

After yet another denial, I was leaving a bank downtown and held the door open for a man coming in. He thanked me and asked, "How are you, young man?"

"Not good—I just got turned down again for a loan."

"Oh, who turned you down?"

"The guy over there in the brown suit," I said, pointing.

"How much money did you need?" he asked. I told him the amount. "Come with me," he said.

I started working in the jewelry business while still in college and soon got the idea of owning my own store. Rinaldi Jewelry opened in 1980 and was located at East 9th Street and Euclid Avenue until 2004, when we moved the business to Solon.

We walked over to the loan officer's desk, and the man said, "Open an account for Mr. Rinaldi for the amount he requested."

It turned out that man was the bank's president, and while he didn't know me personally, he knew someone who worked with my brother and that's why he intervened on my behalf. I was—and still am—grateful for that kind intervention. My father was right: I had a mouth, and I had to use it. That bank was just a few blocks from where my store eventually opened, so I ended up seeing the man frequently and we became friends. One day, he asked if I liked fishing. He explained that he was a member of the well-known Pine Lake Trout Club, and asked if I would like to visit. I gladly accepted the invitation. He said he would pick me up, and we could drive together. Eager to get into the spirit, I dressed in quintessential fishing attire—jeans, a flannel shirt, a fishing hat—and brought my rod and a fully stocked tackle box. When my host pulled up, I was shocked. He was wearing a suit! I quickly concluded he would change into more appropriate clothing at the club. We arrived, and as he got out of the car, he put his tie into his jacket pocket and laid his coat on the back seat. He pulled out a fly rod and started putting it together. "This will just take a minute, and then we can start fishing," he said, still not seeming to mind that I was dressed like a bum. I learned that dressing up was common among the fisherman at the club, who often went there straight from work, still in their business attire. I felt out of place all day but made the best of it!

There were so many fish that you could practically walk across them in the pond. I started casting, and every cast reeled in a fish. After I had caught several, a guy fishing nearby said to me, "You're not a member, are you?"

"No, I came with my friend," and pointed his way.

"Well, you probably should know, your friend has to pay for every fish you catch."

After that, most of the fish I reeled in managed to wriggle off the hook as I picked them up out of the water.

Jewelry Store Hijinks

I proudly opened my jewelry store, Rinaldi Jewelry, at 2028 East 9th Street in Cleveland on December 8, 1980. It happened to be the same day John Lennon was shot and killed. The TV station, WJW, had promised a cover story on the grand opening, but unfortunately, with Lennon's shooting taking precedence in the news, my store's opening didn't receive the coverage I had hoped for. I typically kept my jewelry business separate from my TV career, but in hindsight, I wish I had done more to combine the two for better advertising and to leverage my celebrity status.

I loved having my own store. I was in complete control, and

Flirting with a girl who worked at the store. My lawyer assured me that since we were married, it wasn't sexual harassment.

it gave me a much better work-life balance than the twelve-hour days I had put in at Cowell & Hubbard. My store was open from 10 to 6, which, by comparison, felt like working half a day.

Sherry worked at the jewelry store alongside me. She would get the kids off to school, then come to the store. She kept the books, wrote the checks, and even helped with sales when it was busy. There were no ranks at a store as small as ours; everyone pitched in to do whatever was needed.

I hired my father as head of security. Well, that might be an over-exaggeration. My father enjoyed hanging out at the store, wearing a suit, and talking with the customers and me. After he had been doing that for a while, I bestowed that title upon him. He was great with customers, greeting them when they came in. I never had to buy one paper product for the store because, oddly, my father regularly stocked it with toilet paper, Kleenex, and paper towels. Plus, I don't think my mother minded having him out of the house several hours a day.

Another "hire" I made was a former coworker from Cowell and Hubbard who had retired. Jerry always said he would work for me if I ever opened my own store. Like my father, Jerry just showed up to hang out. He couldn't wrap a jewelry gift box to save his life, but he was one of the best salesmen I've ever worked with. Although we never formalized his position, he began selling so much jewelry that I had to start paying him.

Because the store was located in the heart of downtown, something exciting or at least interesting was always happening. One afternoon a guy walked in dressed like a clown, complete with a big red nose and oversized shoes. Curious, I asked him where he was going. I assumed he was off to entertain kids at a birthday party. He replied, "I have to go to the IRS office to see those clowns, so I thought I'd dress appropriately for the occasion."

A bus driver regularly stopped his bus in front of our store—with passengers on board—and came inside to give us a watermelon from the West Side Market. Cleveland's Finest often stopped by the store to say hello, check on things, and use our bathroom because it was the cleanest in town. Given the nature of our business, I was happy to have the police stop by as often as they liked. Once, a mounted officer even brought his horse into the store—a real accomplishment considering how narrow the place was. Another time, while a mounted cop was using our bathroom, his horse broke free from where it was tied in the alley. Seeing him sprint down East 9th Street after the horse was like one of our comedy skits come to life. And then there was the time we heard strange noises from the back room and thought a burglar had broken in—only to discover it was just a police walkie-talkie chattering, left behind by a patrolman who had stopped to use the bathroom.

A few years after the store opened, a friend stopped in to tell me he was going on vacation. I sighed and told him I wished I could take a vacation.

"Why don't you?" he replied.

"I can't. I have to be here at the store."

"John, when you're on your deathbed and I'm sitting next to you, are you going to say, 'I sure am glad I worked those two weeks'?"

That was some of the best advice I've ever received. I went home that night, and Sherry and I started planning a trip to Aruba. On my deathbed, I wanted to say, "I sure am glad I got that tan!"

An early ad for Rinaldi Jewelry. Something was always going on at East 9th Street and Euclid Avenue, which kept things interesting. We had visits from a bus driver, Cleveland Police officers, a horse, and the occasional crook.
(Cleveland Public Library)

ON WITH THE SHOW

From Sidekick to Spotlight

By 1979, Big Chuck, Hoolihan, Art Lofredo, and I were the Mount Rushmore of the *Hoolihan and Big Chuck Show*. Then, Hoolihan announced he was leaving—moving to Florida. Chuck faced a pivotal decision: Should he end the show . . . or find a new co-host? (I don't think Chuck ever considered hosting alone.) As Chuck quietly contemplated the show's future, he never said a word to me about it.

I was plenty busy, with twelve-hour workdays at Cowell & Hubbard and with my family. I was at Cowell & Hubbard when I received an unexpected call from Bill Flynn, the station manager at TV8. He wanted to see me in his office at the station.

Oh boy, what did I do wrong? I thought.

Although by now I knew most people around the TV station, I was rarely in the building and almost never visited the third floor, where the executive offices were. When I arrived there, I was directed to Bill's office. He got straight to the point.

"Hey, kid, you want to co-host the show with Chuck? He wants you to take over for Bob."

The offer was a complete surprise, but I didn't hesitate to accept.

Pleased with my response, Bill told me to go down the hall and give an interview to Ray Hart, the *Plain Dealer*'s TV columnist. (He wrote a lovely article about me taking over as co-host.) When I left the station I was sky-high, and I rushed back to the jewelry store to call Sherry. She knew I hadn't been making much money

On the set of The Big Chuck & Lil' John Show. When Chuck asked me to become co-host in 1979 it was a complete surprise—but I didn't hesitate to say yes. (I did forget to ask how much it paid, though.) *(Fox8)*

from my work on the show, so she asked me about the pay. In all the excitement, it hadn't occurred to me to ask Bill Flynn any questions. (I didn't find out how much I was paid until I received my first paycheck in the mail.) And it was only weeks later that I learned the name of the new show: *The Big Chuck & Lil' John Show.*

At 11:30 p.m. on Friday, September 7, 1979, Chuck and I hit the airwaves for our first official show as co-hosts, screening the classic *Godzilla vs. the Smog Monster.* I didn't approach my new role any differently from my parts in the skits. I just showed up and did my thing. Although Chuck never mentioned it to me, I know he was initially uneasy. Bob "Hoolihan" Wells was a seasoned professional with years of experience as a TV weatherman, commercial actor, voice-over artist, and community theater performer. Chuck knew that, no matter what on-air disaster might arise, Bob was his safety net and could handle any situation.

I always felt comfortable in front of an audience or a camera, so I knew we had nothing to worry about. And I had complete faith in Chuck's talent. By the time we teamed up, Chuck had already been on the air for more than fifteen years, including his time doing skits with Ernie Anderson on *Shock Theater*, and he was terrific. But I'm not sure Chuck gave himself enough credit, at least not back then. He wasn't just the brains behind the show's execution; he was also fantastic in front of the camera. He just needed time to realize it. With each show his confidence grew as we found our rhythm together.

Mr. Inside and Mr. Outside

Chuck treated me as a fifty-fifty partner from the start and always asked for my opinion, but the show was Chuck's baby. I always referred to him as "Mr. Inside." When it came to anything related to the show, he was the boss and that was fine with me. I was "Mr. Outside," handling all matters related to public appearances and commercial endorsements, as well as managing external relationships.

Chuck's main job at the station was serving as a director and producer for several afternoon and early evening programs, including the news. In addition to those full-time responsibilities, he oversaw all the weekly preparation and pre-production for our show—a massive undertaking that consumed much of his free time.

He developed the skit ideas, wrote the scripts, coordinated all the filming logistics—including props, locations, and people—and even helped build and paint the sets. With almost no budget, Chuck did whatever needed to be done. He didn't have a choice.

As loose as the show sometimes looked, Chuck meticulously scripted it with no room for ad-libs. He orchestrated everything down to the timing of the laughs—except for a tiny rebellion. I discovered that Chuck didn't like being called Charles or Charlie. Naturally, as someone who loved to stir the pot, I occasionally called him Charles on-air, saying his name with the best aristocratic inflection I could muster. He hated it!

On taping day, Chuck could be seen pushing his shopping cart through the halls, script in hand, the cart filled with props, and pulling the necessary audio tapes for the various cues needed for the show. No task was delegated; he didn't trust anyone to get the details right. Despite having successfully completed hundreds of shows, Chuck was always nervous on the day we taped and remained so throughout the entire process until it aired. Even then, he made sure he was in front of a TV when the show aired in case anything went wrong.

When I arrived at the studio on recording days, I'd enter through the back door and head straight to the soundstage. I didn't have much to do other than get my mic pinned on.

Jim Szymanski—our resident "Poor Man's Ed McMahon," as Chuck liked to call him—was responsible for bringing the audience up from the lobby.

Our studio audience was at first a mix of family, friends, and fans. But as the show's popularity grew, we started seeing more organized groups show up, like Boy Scout troops and YMCA Indian Princesses or a group of restaurant employees. Having a live audience brought a special energy to the taping. Everyone was there to have a good time, and that mood was infectious. Chuck and I fed off of it.

Jim would get the audience settled into their seats and explain what was going to happen during the taping. I usually had a few minutes to mingle and clown around with the crowd before we started. Once the cameras were rolling, Chuck and Jim would provide direction, cueing the audience to laugh or cheer at the appropriate time.

A still photo taken during filming of the first Big Chuck & Lil' John Show promotional spot, August 8th 1979. Chuck loved pulling my strings, and I loved yanking his chain whenever I could. *(Fox8)*

A funny note about Jim. For the longest time, I assumed he was a station employee. It wasn't until several years later that I learned Jim was actually a volunteer. He showed up every single week for about forty years without a paycheck, simply because he loved being part of the show.

The actual taping of the show was the least time-consuming part for both of us. Our routine was straightforward: a quick rehearsal of each segment, followed by recording. We could tape a show and have it in the can in under ninety minutes. All I had to do was show up on time, get my mic pinned, and read from the teleprompter. (I often silently thanked my third-grade teacher, Mrs. Ryan, for teaching me to read.)

For the first year or so, we taped during the afternoon. I was still working at Cowell & Hubbard, so we taped during my lunch hour. I'd go downtown to pick up jewelry from our main store on Euclid Avenue to bring back to the Cleveland Heights store—and stop at the station in between. That's why I was dressed so well in those early shows—I didn't have time to change out of my suit. Not many people knew, but the large briefcase that sat just off-camera next to me while we recorded was filled with jewelry. I was responsible for its safekeeping so it never left my sight. As soon as we finished taping and signing a few autographs, I would quickly exit the back door of the station, the same way I had come in, and head back to work.

We changed our schedule after about a year and began taping at 7 p.m., after the early evening news. I would leave the jewelry store at 5 p.m., go to a restaurant for dinner, and then to the studio for taping.

The camaraderie viewers saw between Chuck and me on TV was genuine. We enjoyed working together and became close friends. We had a lot in common. We were both devoted family men, had an overachieving work ethic, and came from ethnic backgrounds—Chuck, of Polish descent, and me, of Italian descent. We shared many common interests, like our love for cooking. But we also had distinct differences. In his spare time, Chuck enjoyed mowing the lawn and grocery shopping, neither of which I'm fond of.

Although Chuck and I got along well, we had very different personalities, as was evident to anyone watching the show. I was high-energy, a risk-taker, fearless, and often impulsive. Chuck was methodical, contemplative, and deliberate. Whenever I started to ramble or veer off on a tangent, Chuck would reel me back in. Then I sometimes pushed him to go in directions he wouldn't have explored on his own. We created a dynamic balance, and I believe

In the early days of the show, we taped during my lunch breaks from work at Cowell & Hubbard jewelry store, so I was usually wearing a suit. And just off-camera was usually a briefcase filled with valuable jewelry. *(Fox8)*

those differences were crucial to our success. A reporter once told me, "The difference between you and Chuck is, if you were handed a mic right on the spot and told to go live on national TV, you'd just do it. Chuck would have to think about it—but after ten minutes, he'd do it way better."

Chuck liked to do things his way. That never bothered me—well, except for one little thing. Back when people still wrote and mailed letters, we might receive as many as sixty letters a week, and more during the summer when the kids were out of school. Chuck was in charge of opening the mail. Whenever he received a request for a public appearance or a commercial, he would call me at the jewelry store to read the entire letter to me. I'd jot down information I might need when later calling to follow up on the request. That was fine, except we might get several personal-appearance request letters on the same day. Each letter, he called again—maybe even just a few minutes after I had just spoken to him about the previous one. We might repeat this process several times. I finally told him, "Read all the letters, then call me, and we can go through all of them on one phone call." He didn't like that idea. "Okay," I said. "I see you at least three times a week. Put the letters on the corner of your desk, and we can go through them when I'm in the studio." He replied "It's not my nature to put work aside." And, he said, he didn't like leaving papers on his desk because he feared the cleaning staff would throw them away. That was Chuck!

I Sing, People Suffer

Although I was a different sort of co-host from Hoolihan, with my own personality and sense of humor, the overall format of the show remained the same—except for one small change. Viewers had always sent in pictures of themselves or their loved ones, and toward the end of the show, birthdays were recognized by showing the photos while Hoolihan and Chuck sang "Happy Birthday." When I took over, my off-key singing was so awful that Chuck canceled the singing portion. Instead, the segment featured the recordings "Happy Happy Birthday, Baby" by the Tune Weavers and "Sixteen Candles" by the Crests. I have no illusions about my singing abilities. Compared to my voice, nails on a chalkboard sound good. But I was determined to bring the singing portion back. I began taking professional singing lessons every Friday before work. For a year and a half, I stuck with it. However, about six weeks in, it became clear that my singing wasn't improving. After one lesson, the building's janitor stopped me in the hall and said, "Hey, buddy, I think you're wasting your money." But I wasn't discouraged. I was having such a great time that I kept showing up. We eventually stopped trying to improve my singing and just spent the time belting out show tunes. To this day, my singing sends cats running for cover.

One of the show's funniest and most embarrassing moments happened during one of the pajama parties at the end of the show. A woman from the Red Cross came on to demonstrate the Heimlich maneuver. Chuck, in order to demonstrate what *not* to do, grabbed me and flipped me upside down—and my pajamas slid up completely, exposing my underwear. Thank goodness I was wearing some!

Dynamic Duo

Chuck and I followed a time-honored formula for a comedy duo: the straight man and the clown. We were in the tradition of Abbott and Costello, Laurel and Hardy, Martin and Lewis, and many others. We stuck to our respective roles on the show, and Chuck wrote our parts in the skits with this in mind. (I played the clown, in case you weren't sure.)

One way to identify my earliest skits is that I usually had a cigar in my hand or mouth. I even actually *smoked* a cigar on set in the beginning—something unheard of today. For my first co-hosted show, the opening skit was Chuck's idea, as most of them were. In it, I was perched on an elevated stage, playing a military general. I delivered my lines with all the sternness I could muster, announcing that Hoolie was gone and there would be no crying. At the end of the skit, a cleaning lady (played by Mary Allen) pushed me off the stage. I flipped headfirst into a laundry basket—with a concrete floor beneath. After the dive, I lay still for a moment, and Linda, our camera operator (whom we affectionately called Mama Linda) quipped, "I think he's dead!" I was fearless and willing to do anything for a skit—young and dumb.

When it came to filming, I trusted Chuck completely. I did what he asked without question. He was meticulous in planning and took every safety precaution he could. Even after we retired, if Chuck had asked me to jump through a window, my young mind would have done it without hesitation, although my older body might have argued.

Despite careful planning, we still had a few injuries while filming hundreds of skits.

During a kung fu skit, Chuck kept urging me to hit him harder, so I finally gave him a solid hit—and broke his ribs. In the skit "Looney Legends," inspired by Gulliver's Travels, Chuck was tied up on the ground, and I was supposed to be a Lilliputian crawling on top of him and falling off his chest. To create the effect, we used a green screen and I crawled on the bleachers we used for audience seating—to be combined later with an image of Chuck lying on the ground. Chuck arranged everything carefully, including cushions to break my fall as I tumbled off the bleachers. Unfortunately, someone moved one of the cushions, and I hit my face on the hard bleacher. My lip split open, and blood gushed everywhere. One of the directors rushed in on-camera, which killed the shot, and I had to redo it. I took several attempts at the reshoot because my lip was throbbing, and I was apprehensive after the accident.

We did a takeoff of the John Belushi *Saturday Night Live* skit "The Samurai Weatherman." I played the director of a news broadcast, and Rick, one of the producers at WJW, played the samurai and threw me through the weather map. Unfortunately, he threw me too far, past the cushions and into the concrete floor. No serious injuries, but I was a little banged up.

While shooting another skit, I was walking through a car

With Chuck in his office, getting ready to tape the show. I never had my own space at the station. I referred to Chuck as "Mr. Inside." When it came to the show, he was the boss and that was fine with me. I was "Mr. Outside," handling public appearances and endorsements. *(Bill Ward)*

wash when my long keychain got caught in the big brush, and it started to pick me up. Just as I began to panic, the chain broke—fortunately before any harm was done.

Despite a few cuts and bruises, I was relatively unharmed throughout. I can't say the same for my suits, though. I ruined many suits shooting skits. During a stop-motion skit in which Chuck and I were "driving" around town by scooting across the pavement on our butts instead of using actual cars, the constant sliding destroyed the seat of my suit pants. After ruining several pairs of pants, I finally wised up and had leather patches sewn into the seat.

In the "That's Incredible" strongest jaws skit, a dummy of Chuck is dropped from above and falls on me. While filming, I hit the ground and tore my brand-new suit pants and jacket sleeves.

In an ice-skating skit, I was showing off and split my pants right down the middle. I lost yet another pair of pants when I fell to the ground while shooting a skit outside the Crazy Horse saloon. We filmed a skit where I ate at a restaurant and complained to the waiter (Chuck) about a fly in my soup. Instead of bringing me a fresh bowl, Chuck decides to spray bug repellent directly into my soup. We shot it two ways. In the second version, Chuck grabs a fly swatter and swings at the fly, causing soup to splatter all over me. I didn't lose that suit, but I was stuck with a heavy dry-cleaning bill. In all, I am sure I laid at least a dozen suits to rest. Better that I lost some pants rather than limbs.

Two Thousand Skits

We made so many skits that sometimes now I'll see one I don't remember taping. Some memories stand out, though. I couldn't see for about an hour after shooting a skit we called "Certain Ethnic Flashbulb Tester." Once, while playing Little Miss Muffet in one of our "Fractured Fairy Tales" skits, when the spider was lowered down on a fishing line, I grabbed the spider, shoved it in my mouth, and started chewing. I didn't realize it was attached to the line with a metal pin—which went straight into my mouth. While playing a monk ringing a bell in a cathedral, the shoot took forever because the bell kept landing wrong. When it fell on me, it either tipped over or landed crooked. We once filmed a skit with a local guy selected because he matched my height and was perfect for the role. Unfortunately, we had to stop showing the skit shortly after it first aired because he got arrested for robbing a bank.

I'll never forget filming the fish store skit. In the scene, a couple enters the store looking to buy goldfish. Instead of using a net, like a normal person, I jump into the tank to catch the fish. It was a fifty-gallon tank—plenty large enough for me to fit inside and

This classic photo was used maybe a thousand times to promote *The Big Chuck and Lil' John Show.* I still like it. That was a great tux! *(Fox8)*

move around. What I didn't anticipate was the water temperature. For some reason, I assumed it would be warm. It wasn't! When I hit the water, it felt like I'd jumped into a frozen lake. By the time I climbed out, I was freezing and completely drenched—fully dressed, including my "certain ethnic sweater." (Speaking of the certain ethnic sweater, I got mine from a fan who had washed and shrunk it, so he sent it to me knowing it would fit.)

Chuck and I did an admirable job recreating the famous Abbott and Costello "Who's on First" skit. It wasn't hard; we filmed it in separate takes with cue cards just off-camera. For the audio engineer skit (one of our most requested), I practiced for hours in my basement. I ran up and down the ladder until I had everything just right. When it was time to shoot, I nailed it in one take. I was painted green for a Jolly Green Giant skit. Chuck assured me the paint would wash right off. It didn't, and I was green everywhere for a week. And had to go to work at the jewelry store looking like a giant string bean.

In several early skits I can be seen standing on an upright bass—the way rockabilly musicians would actually stand on the instrument while playing it. The idea came from watching the bass player in a friend's band. After the show, I told him how cool that was. He said it took practice, but if I wanted to learn, he had an old bass I could borrow, so I did. The upright bass has a balance point where it can stand on its own. Climbing onto it was all about finding and maintaining that sweet spot.

I don't have a favorite skit, but if forced to choose, it would be "The Troglodyte," my fourth skit. It was memorable because it was my breakout skit that captured fans' attention—and also because I nearly drowned. I was supposed to run down the boat ramp at Hinckley Lake and splash into the water, but the depth suddenly changed from six inches to six feet, and I couldn't swim. Thankfully, Chuck's son, Michael, jumped in and pulled me out. After that, anytime we shot a skit in water deeper than I was tall, I was tethered to Chuck's leg with a rope. Despite having some lessons, I never learned how to swim. Perhaps it has something to do with muscle density—who knows?—but I sink.

Most of my immediate family appeared in at least one skit. My father made a cameo in a Ben Crazy skit. Chuck's mother and my mother both starred in a skit along with Channel 8 weatherman Dick Goddard. In the scene, two older ladies were supposed to throw snowballs at Dick. The problem was, neither of our mothers could throw. We filmed the skit with Chuck and me just off camera as the "designated throwers," firing snowballs at Dick. We nailed him pretty good, and to his credit Dick took it all in stride.

My sons, Dino and Johnny, both appeared in a few skits over the years. In one, the scene opens with them taking turns telling Santa what they want for Christmas. Then it's my turn. I'm dressed as a kid, and when I sit on Santa's lap I innocently ask if I can have a copy of his naughty girls list. Dino also starred in a skit in which he was swinging on a swing while a pretty young girl sunbathed on the other side of a nearby fence. I hilariously kick Dino off his swing so I can use it to get a better view of the pretty girl. Dino ended up being featured in more skits, but Johnny had his moment in the spotlight: he landed a role in *The Wandering Muse of Artemis Flagg,* the movie Chuck directed starring Burgess Meredith.

We filmed a new skit almost every week, so Chuck was constantly under pressure to come up with new material. Some skits were quick fillers and not Chuck's best ideas, but they worked well enough until he came up with a better idea the following week. Even when these stinkers aired, we'd still announce them on-air as one of our favorites.

Chuck had his hands full coordinating everything—costumes, props, sets, and actors. If a skit needed a firehouse, a bathtub full of sponges, a microscope, or a dozen helium-filled balloons, that fell on Chuck. He would arrange for garbage trucks, forklifts, a Greyhound bus, or horses when needed. With special effects, Chuck was ahead of his time. Many skits were filmed with early split-screen, green-screen, and superimposition techniques. He did these things not only because he was creative, but also because it was necessary to get the shots he wanted with a small budget. The low budgets made the skits more work to pull off and stretched Chuck's creative abilities.

We made roughly two thousand skits. Six of them were my idea. And I'm sticking to the story that they were six of our best. "Half a Head of Lettuce" with Chuck and Big Stash was one of those, though I borrowed the concept from a Flip Wilson performance I saw in Las Vegas ("... and this fine gentleman would like the other half"). I also told Chuck about the sword-stuck-in-the-stone bit from my grade-school play. In our version I lie on my back and use my feet to kick the stone off the blade—and then the stone comes crashing down on my head, knocking me out cold.

I had two ideas that Chuck didn't like, so we never did them. We often did special shows with themes, like "Lil' John Night" or "Oldies Night." I wanted to do a special show featuring skits of people who had passed away and call it "Dead Night." Chuck felt it was too morbid and not right for our audience. I am sure he was right. The other idea Chuck vetoed, which I do think would have been fun, was a show featuring Dick Goddard, Art Lofredo, Chuck, and me as old men in the future. Picture Dick on a walker, Art in a wheelchair, Chuck and me with gray hair, welcoming everyone into the breaks as geriatric greeters. We'd all be reminiscing about the good old days while trying to remember where we left our glasses and reminding each other to take our pills. I guess Chuck thought it was too silly, but I still think it would've been a hilarious way to show that we never wanted to grow up and we had kept our sense of humor.

You Can Be Sick Later

I'm sure you've heard the old showbiz adage, "The show must go on." That was our mantra. By the time I was co-hosting, the show was being pre-recorded. (In the early years, Chuck had done it live.) But we still had the pressure to deliver a new show every week. We taped on Thursday, and the show had to be ready for airing Friday night, which didn't leave much time for error. Thursday was not the day to stop by Chuck's office for idle chit-chat. He was deep in "the zone," laser-focused on last-minute details, ensuring everything was ready for the cameras. When I arrived at the studio, I might stop by his office to let him know I was there or to say a simple hello, but aside from that, I did my best to stay out of his hair.

In all those years, we never missed a show—sick, dying, or dead, we taped. I often urged Chuck to record a backup episode, just in case, but we never did. Looking back, I wish we had, because there were times when one of us was so sick I wasn't sure we'd make it through. There was one occasion when Chuck was so ill that we had to pause between segments so he could throw up in a bucket.

Once, in the 1980s, Chuck asked Dick Goddard to fill in when he was in the hospital and couldn't make the taping. That didn't stop Chuck from being involved, though. He still wrote the script and even prerecorded a segment that aired. I stopped by the hospital to pick up the script, and when I entered his room, the scene was grim: Chuck was covered from head to toe in a white sheet, and the doctor stood over his bed, looking somber. Without missing a beat, I told the doctor, "If he's dead, don't say a word. We'll stuff him, prop him up on the set, and I'll keep this thing going for at least another three years." Chuck burst into laughter. He had heard me coming down the hall greeting the nurses, and he couldn't resist the chance for a good prank.

Chuck was just as die-hard about public appearances as he was about the show. He once broke his arm during an All-Stars game, yet insisted on finishing the game before heading to the hospital. I had my own share of near-misses. I was deathly ill for an event at Aurora Woodlands, near SeaWorld, that, in hindsight, we should have canceled. We pushed through three shows that day, with the final running from 10 p.m. to midnight. As soon as it wrapped up, I rushed to the bathroom to vomit, completely forgetting I had a hot mic. The crowd heard everything—but assumed it was part of the act and laughed as I crouched over the toilet, heaving.

Cleveland's Enough for Me

Although Chuck was employed by WJW as a director and producer, neither of us was under contract for *The Big Chuck & Lil' John Show*. Each quarter, the station released its upcoming show schedule for the next three months, and each time I anxiously checked to see if we were still on it. For the entire run of the show, we never knew for sure how much longer we would be on the air. That uncertainty is one reason why I never considered leaving the jewelry business for a showbiz career, at least not seriously.

When I first began performing on *The Hoolihan and Big Chuck Show* in the early 1970s, before I was married, I told *Plain Dealer* entertainment columnist Ray Hart that I wanted to be the next Bob Hope and had given myself two years to make it. But while my appearances on the show became more frequent, that was the only work I did in the entertainment business. Years later, after becoming the show's co-host and winning several Emmys, I called Ernie "Ghoulardi" Anderson, who had gone on from Channel 8 to make a name for himself in California as the iconic network voice-over guy for ABC. I asked him about pursuing a career in Hollywood. He said, "You could make it out here, John, but you have to be out here. There are twenty guys like you out here already, and no one from California is calling Cleveland." It was a fleeting thought, and I quickly reached the same conclusion Chuck had years earlier: I didn't want to leave Cleveland or uproot my family.

Locally, there wasn't enough opportunity or money in TV to make me consider leaving the jewelry business. I was doing very well and loved being my own boss. However, had I known the TV show would endure as long as it did, I might have made a different choice—maybe selling jewelry by private appointment instead of opening a store. Besides Sherry and me, our store had minimal staff, and the responsibilities of operating it took much of my time.

I turned down many invitations for paid speaking engagements and personal appearances because of my duties at the store.

Detroit Didn't Get Us

Bill Flynn asked Chuck and me to pilot our show in Detroit. Bill had been the general manager and vice president of WJW TV8 in Cleveland, but left for a management role at a sister station in Detroit. He loved our show and thought we could replicate our success in Detroit.

In May 1983, we went on the air in Detroit. It was a thirteen-week trial run. Thirteen weeks has always been a significant milestone for TV shows. If a show lasted that long, it had a good chance of being picked up for another season. (After moving from Cleveland to California, Tim Conway had a license plate on his car that read "13WKS".)

Chuck and I would leave for Detroit right after we finished our day jobs in Cleveland. We usually arrived early, giving us time to relax before taping began at 7 p.m. In the middle of taping, the crew would pause and disappear for fifteen minutes without saying a word to Chuck or me. This happened several times, and I eventually asked where everyone had gone. Turns out there was free coffee and snacks down the hall. That would have been nice to know on day one! But I get it—we were new to the station, and it takes time to build relationships. Even after several weeks, though, we never really connected with the staff. It was a distinctly different atmosphere from the family-like one we had back in Cleveland.

It was also clear from the start that our humor didn't land with the Detroit audience. The stack of negative review letters at the studio confirmed it. It didn't help that most of the live audience the Detroit station brought it in didn't speak—or understand—

English. I don't know where they found them. We relied on audience reactions to bring energy to the show, and without that the jokes just fell flat.

The Detroit experiment ended after our thirteen-week contract. It was probably for the best. It was a lot of traveling. Once we finished taping at about 9 p.m., we drove home. I would have preferred to stay overnight, but Chuck was adamant about returning each night. He wanted to be home with his family and in his own bed. We were driving back and forth such a long distance on the same day, and we were both tired; I was worried we might end up in a serious accident. I saw Chuck more than I saw my family, and we spent so much time together, especially on those long road trips, that we sometimes ran out of things to discuss. To pass the time, I'd set up little statues on the car's dashboard and knock one over at specific mile markers. After knocking over so many statues, we'd treat ourselves to a snack. That might have been the most exciting part of the entire Detroit experience. On one trip back, we got stopped by the highway patrol. After explaining to the cop who we were, he kindly let us go and said, "Mention on your show that the highway patrol are good guys, and that you got a break in Michigan."

And the Emmy Goes to . . .

In Cleveland we were setting record ratings and winning industry awards. By 1984, our popularity was so strong that we launched a second show, on Saturday afternoons. Our popularity remained so high that we were asked to star in a pizza commercial that aired during the Super Bowl in the 1990s (the exact year escapes me). How many people can say that? Chuck and I were nominated for several Emmys, but it wasn't until the third nomination that we finally scored. Chuck had previously won Emmy awards for his

With Sherry and one of my twelve Emmy awards. After you win an Emmy, I noticed, people treat you differently. Well, some people anyway.

work before we teamed up, but this was a first for us together—and a first for me—and it felt great.

The awards show that year was at the Cleveland Play House. After receiving an award, recipients exited through a side door and returned to their seats with the rest of the audience. On my way back, some guy stopped me in the hall and asked if I'd won an Emmy. I proudly held up my award and said, "I did!" He responded snidely, "Anyone can win one." Talk about a buzz kill! The next year, Chuck and I won again. I saw that same guy, and walked up to him. "That's two," I said, holding up two fingers and my Emmy in the other hand.

I went on to win twelve Emmys. Chuck took home twenty-nine, including Best Director and Best Producer awards. It's incredible to think—forty-one Emmys between us! Whenever I won, I felt I was on top of the world. While the initial rush fades, a lasting sense of pride remains: Lil' John Rinaldi—Emmy Winner. And although it's not talked about, winning an Emmy influences how others in the industry treat you, especially those who have earned their own.

SPORTS FAN

A Lesson from Dad

I've been a Cleveland sports fan my entire life. My father and I went to many games together and always had great seats. Once, at a baseball game when I was a kid, a foul ball was hit near us. My father could have easily caught it, but he didn't move. When I asked him why, he said, "It's just a baseball." I guess he didn't feel it was worth messing up his suit trying to catch it. This was still when men dressed in suits for the game. After the game, my father leaned toward the dugout and said, "Hey Joe, give me a couple of baseballs, will ya?" It was very thoughtful of my dad to get the balls, but my eight-year-old mind couldn't help thinking it wasn't the same as catching one.

The Cleveland Arena, on Euclid Avenue near East 36th Street, was where my dad and I saw many boxing matches, which were hugely popular in the 1950s, '60s, and '70s. My dad always taught me never to sit in the front row. "If you sit a few rows back, you can duck behind the guy in front of you and avoid getting hit with blood and sweat, without ruining your suit." He was right. This tip was helpful years later when my buddies and I went to female mud wrestling matches.

Surviving Mike Tyson

Anytime boxing is mentioned, I can't help but think about September 2, 1989, the day when Chuck and I fought heavyweight champion Mike Tyson. Mike is one of the biggest celebrities I have ever met. I've noticed that the bigger the celebrity, the nicer they tend to be. The event was a charity exhibition organized by George Forbes and Fannie Lewis, longtime Cleveland city council members, with promoter Don King. We held a private rehearsal at George Forbes's office for the upcoming press conference, with Chuck and me, local radio hosts Gary Dee and Lynn Tolliver, and Mike Tyson in attendance. Each of us would be in the ring with Tyson for three one-minute rounds. Chuck and I would go together. During rehearsal, Tyson said to Gary Dee and Lynn Tolliver, "I'm not going to hurt you guys. You're an old man, and you're a fat fool." But then he turned to Chuck: "You're a big man, I'm gonna hurt you." Then he looked at me: "I'm gonna knock you out."

The public press conference drew a crowd, including ESPN reporters. It was a significant event for Cleveland and us. Chuck and I planned a gag for the press conference that no one else knew about. Once Don King began talking, I would get agitated and jump across the table at Tyson while Chuck held me back by my belt. Tyson didn't know me and was genuinely shocked when I lunged at him, but then he and Don King laughed. "You're not a champ; you're a chump," I told Tyson throughout the event. Something that amused me then—and still does—is that even though Tyson could have cleared a room with one hand, he always had a bodyguard.

Before the fight, on our show, we aired video clips of our training routine—Chuck hitting a side of beef in a meat packing plant and me working over frozen chickens in a chicken factory.

The fight itself took place at John Adams High School, my alma mater. To make it extra memorable, Chuck and I arrived by helicopter. We flew over Cleveland and circled the Terminal Tower before landing at our destination. Gary Dee and Lynn Tolliver were scheduled to fight first, and Chuck and I were the grand finale. Gary didn't show up for the fight, and Lynn went to the

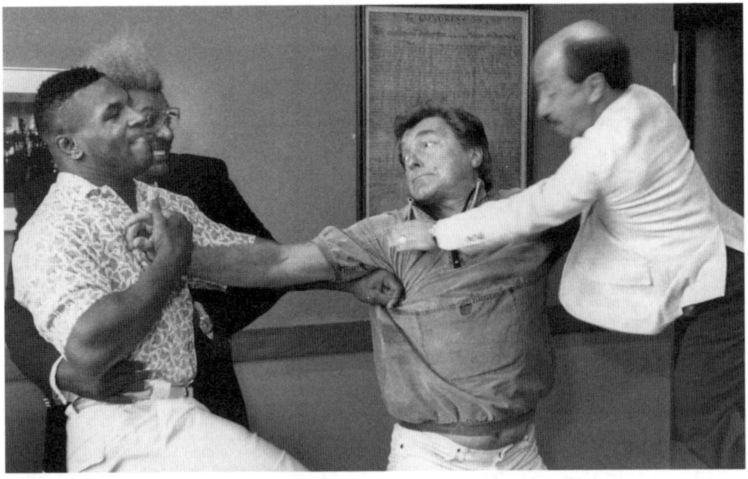

During our pre-fight press conference I genuinely shocked heavyweight champ Mike Tyson. Luckily, he didn't kill me. *(Cleveland Public Library)*

middle of the ring and just lay down. I couldn't tell if he was scared or being funny.

Our turn came, and we made a grand entrance into the ring, with loudspeakers blasting "Gonna Fly Now," the theme from *Rocky*. Kevin Salyer, the marketing and promotions manager of WJW, was the ring announcer. Chuck was introduced first, and I was announced as "the Italian Pony." The referee searched Chuck and me, and the crowd roared when he removed several weapons from my clothes, including a hammer and a horseshoe.

Humor aside, we had actually been working out with experienced trainers for several weeks and were decked out in full professional boxing gear for the exhibition. I told my trainer, Cecil, I'd love to land one punch. He advised me that Tyson would step back when I went in to punch him—something he wouldn't do in a real fight. The idea was to follow up quickly if Tyson stepped back. But I wasn't fooling this champion; he was ready for everything I threw at him. He dodged and ducked effortlessly. I did manage to hit him once, but it was like throwing a Wiffle Ball against a

I've got heavyweight champ Tyson right where I want him. *(Don Nottage, City of Cleveland photographer)*

brick wall. Tyson tagged Chuck good in the first round, leaving him sore for days. He hit me once, and I rolled across the canvas like a tumbleweed. At one point, Tyson lifted me upside down, and I worried he might toss me over his shoulder and break my back. Thankfully, he knew exactly what he was doing, and Chuck and I left the ring alive.

Tyson wasn't the only heavyweight champion I had the pleasure of meeting. Once, late at night after a personal appearance, knowing everyone at home would be asleep, I decided to stop by Swingos Keg & Quarter at East 18th and Euclid for a nightcap. Swingos had become the go-to spot after Elvis had booked the hotel during a tour stop in town. That night, the nightclub was bustling. Professional heavyweight boxing champion Larry Holmes was there, and somehow we ended up on stage together, playing the bongos. When I got home, I was still so excited that

I woke Sherry and said, "Guess who I was with tonight? Larry Holmes!"

Half asleep, she replied, "That's great, John. Who's Larry Holmes?"

Black-and-Gold Guardian Angel

For many years I attended Browns-Steelers games in Pittsburgh. Browns fans are undoubtedly dedicated, but Steelers fans are equally passionate about their team. I've heard stories of Steelers fans who included their season tickets in wills and divorce settlements. I attended every Browns-Steelers game for years, enduring countless losses in Pittsburgh's stadium. I witnessed my team lose in every way possible—interceptions, fumbles, you name it. When I attended games, I made no secret that I was a Browns fan, and I've had hot dogs thrown at my feet, been jeered at, and someone in my party was even threatened with having mustard smeared on them if the Browns won. I usually stayed with friends while I was in town for a game, and some of *them* even turned against me and would stop talking to me if Cleveland seemed poised to win.

At one game in Pittsburgh, two fans were jawing at each other when a large man sitting across the aisle stood up and said, "You both better shut up because if you start anything, I'm going to kill both of you." The fans quickly sat back down; this was not the kind of guy you wanted to mess with. I turned to my friend and asked who the man was. My friend explained, "He goes by Armand," and said he was the toughest guy in the stadium. As a Browns fan in a sea of black and gold, I decided Armand was someone I wanted to be on the good side of. The next time the beer guy came around, I sent ten beers to Armand.

At halftime, Armand came over and thanked me. "Are you the

guy from Cleveland?" he asked. "If you need anything, just let me know, and don't worry—no one here is going to bother you. I'll make sure of it."

I saw Armand at games for several years, but one game, I noticed my protector wasn't in his regular seat. That made me a little nervous, but just before the game started, two of the biggest guys I'd ever seen came down the aisle, and one tapped me on the shoulder and said, "Are you the guy from Cleveland? I'm Armand's son. He sent us here to take care of you." After years of losses, the Browns finally ended their losing streak, and I went wild—jumping, yelling, and celebrating the long-awaited victory. After things had settled down and the fans began to leave, the two big guys returned. "Are you good? Is it okay if we leave now?" Thanks for looking out, Armand!

PERSONAL APPEARANCES— CHA CHING!

Dick Goddard to the Rescue

Shortly after filming my first skit, "Bridget the Midget," in 1971, the local actors' union representative called to ask if I wanted to join. I declined. I had no idea if my involvement in the show would continue. About ten minutes later, Chuck called. "Hey John, I heard you refused to join the union," he said.

"I didn't refuse. The guy asked if I wanted to join, and I said no."

Chuck explained that I had to be in the union to continue being part of the show. I called the guy back and told him I would join. It was a decision that later almost made me leave the show. In those early years, I made very little money from the show, and the small checks I received went entirely to the union for dues. About six months later, I got another call from a union representative. "Mr. Rinaldi, you're what we call a slow pay."

I could feel my face instantly turn red with anger. "Slow pay? How about no pay? I am sending the union one hundred percent of my check, and I'm getting nothing! I'm going to call Babe Triscaro." At the time, Louis "Babe" Triscaro was the head of the Teamsters union.

"You know Babe Triscaro?"

"Yeah, I know him quite well, and so does my father, and I'm

Dick Goddard, a.k.a. "Mr. Nice Guy"—and he really was! He was star player on the All-Stars, an occasional actor in skits, and I heard he was a pretty good meteorologist, too. If not for Dick Goddard, I might have quit the show soon after I started.

calling him as soon as we hang up." I never heard from the union rep again.

Later that week, in the hall at the TV station, I was thinking about that call when I ran into Dick Goddard. "How's it going, John?" he asked.

"I don't know, Dick. I'm thinking of quitting the show. I'm making very little money, and I send it all to the union. After paying for parking and gas, I'm losing money on this deal."

"Listen John, from now on, every time I'm asked to do a personal appearance, I'll say I can't go unless they invite you, too."

"Thanks, Dick. I appreciate the offer, but I don't have an act."

Dick laughed. "Neither do I."

Once I began making personal appearances with Dick, the

thought of leaving the show never entered my mind again. If he hadn't made such a generous offer, things might have turned out very differently for both me and Cleveland TV. I would have done anything for my friend after that. Dick seemed to have a sixth sense about me; on more than one occasion, he told me, "Stick around, John. You're the heir apparent."

Personal appearances were routine events and had been a staple for people on the show since 1963, back to the Ghoulardi days. When I first started making appearances with Dick, I quickly developed a short comedy routine of jokes and humorous ways to entertain the crowd. But Dick and I mainly answered fan questions and signed autographs. It was easy work and always a good time.

Not long after, I also began making personal appearances with Chuck, filling in for Hoolihan when he was unavailable—something that became more common as his freelance work out of town increased. One of my earliest appearances with Chuck was at a parade in Mogadore. A city representative approached us, smiling, and said, "I love the show, I watch it all the time, and Lil' Bill, you're the best"—despite standing in front of a huge sign on the parade car that said "Big Chuck & Lil' John."

Magic

When Chuck and I started performing together regularly, our comedy routine was simple, and many of the sketches were borrowed from acts he and Hoolie had done. I'd engage with the audience by sharing things about Big Chuck and myself, such as, "Chuck is married with kids, and I have three kids—one of each." One of our earliest sketches was called "HEP," which stood for "handkerchief, eyeglass, pen." Chuck was blindfolded and I'd tell the audience, "We're so in tune with each other, he can read my

Abracadabra! Our earliest public appearances were pretty basic, but Chuck and I eventually developed a well-organized comedy routine, including a magic act. We always kept it light-hearted and family friendly.

mind." I'd hold an item up and ask Chuck to guess what it was. For example, I'd hold up a handkerchief and say, "Okay, Chuck, what am I holding? Don't *blow* this one." Chuck, of course, knew it was a handkerchief but would guess something wrong, like, "A whistle?" I'd say, "No, try again, *chief!*" Then, he'd guess a handkerchief. Next, I might pick up a small child from the audience and say, "*Boy*, oh *boy*, oh *boy*, can you guess what I have now?" Chuck would guess wrong again. I'd respond with, "Quit *kid*ding around!" Our entertainment was always light-hearted and family-friendly.

Eventually, we developed well-organized comedy routines and

a magic act with various tricks. One of the tricks went like this: Chuck would hold a rod with three handkerchiefs tied to it. I'd tell the audience, "Before your very eyes, Chuck will take the blue cloth from this end and move it to the other end." Chuck would put it behind his back and just twirl it around. I'd say, "I know it's a little fast for some of you . . . let's switch it back." Of course, the kids would start booing the obvious switch. Then I'd ask where they wanted the blue cloth to go, and they'd shout, "In the middle!" So I'd give the rod a tap, and—*voilà!*—the blue cloth would magically appear in the middle.

One nice thing about our act was its versatility—we could adjust it to fit, whether we had fifteen minutes or an hour. And if we needed more time, we would bring people onstage or play a game of TV trivia with prizes. We carried a portable tape player and played recorded tapes of TV theme songs, asking the audience to guess the show.

We performed the same routines in public for so many years that the audiences knew the act as well as we did, and if we missed something, they'd shout, "Hey, what about . . .?" Chuck and I performed together for more than fifty years, and I still incorporate some of our original acts into my appearances today. We both carried a suitcase filled with props and magic tricks to every appearance. I still have most of the props we used back then.

Personal appearances are easy—shaking hands, signing autographs, doing a short comedy routine. But formal speaking engagements are different. Being a keynote speaker means delivering a formal and engaging speech. I can do both, but I'm not a motivational speaker. I consider myself a storyteller. During one of my earliest speaking engagements, while I was still learning the ropes, I told the promoter to have people write down questions, and I would answer them. I only remember one question I couldn't answer: "What is the chemical composition of a ruby?" Which I now know is aluminum oxide.

We Went Everywhere

Chuck and I attended hundreds of festivals, parades, grand openings, and school events. Some events were sponsored by for-profit businesses, and others by charitable causes. Some were official WJW-sponsored events; others Chuck and I arranged ourselves. I've attended thousands of events and personal appearances, with and without Chuck. While many memories blur, they're filled with decades of handshakes, photos, and good times. Event promoters treated us like royalty, and both Chuck and I genuinely loved meeting our fans. But as much fun as we had, we also needed the money. Despite the TV show's popularity, the pay was minimal, and even though both Chuck and I had regular jobs, we had families to support. So when it came to earning extra money, we shared the same mindset: accept any paying opportunity we were offered. If someone called and asked us to stand in the woods during a blizzard for three hours, my response was, "Are we getting paid? Then we'll be there." We rarely had fewer than two events booked each week, and sometimes more. We maintained this rigorous schedule for decades. My favorite four words to hear after an event were "See you next year."

Chuck and I had an explicit agreement regarding our schedule. If Chuck had an obligation, a family birthday for example, and needed a date kept free, he only had to let me know, and I would ensure we didn't book anything for that day. Once a date was set, however, we honored our commitment no matter what. There were only a couple of exceptions that I recall. Chuck understandably missed an event when his wife went into labor with their daughter. I missed one when a jack-knifed tractor-trailer truck shut down I-77. (This was years before cell phones, so I couldn't call anyone from the road to let them know I was delayed.) The following Saturday, at the jewelry store, I shared the story of missing the event with a nice couple I was helping. I mentioned the jack-knifed truck, and without meaning any harm, said, "Some idiot caused a wreck, causing the entire freeway to be shut down." I immediately turned red with embarrassment when the couple I was speaking to admitted they were the ones responsible for that accident.

Haunted house season was always our busiest time of the year. We were booked several nights a week and often double- or triple-booked on Saturdays. Akron's Haunted Schoolhouse and Laboratory was a staple in our annual rotation, and we were there at least one weekend for about twenty-two years. Our slot was typically from 6 to 8 p.m. and part of the proceeds went to charity. The show's promoter insisted that we start *and* finish right on time. We felt terrible having to stop signing autographs while people were still in line. Stationed there with us for many years was an Akron police officer known as the Wolfman because he could howl just like a wolf.

Once we wrapped up an event, we would meet with the organizer to get paid. However, tracking down our payment was sometimes a hassle. There was one event where the promoter would show up at the start, then head to a bar, and we would have to go there to collect. To make things worse, he'd announce that we'd be at the bar at a particular time, which meant the place was packed, stretching our appearance beyond the scheduled time because we couldn't just walk in, get paid, and leave. Most of our appearances involved a formal commitment to show up at a local bar or restaurant afterward, which was fine when it was planned. If it wasn't, that was frustrating because of other commitments we may have had, especially family obligations. Unfortunately, Chuck and I missed many family and personal events due to our busy appearance schedule.

An event that sticks out in my mind is bear wrestling. For charity, I wrestled Victor the bear four times. There was one rule in these matches: I wasn't allowed to jump on his back (which I wouldn't have done anyway). My strategy was simple. Whenever Victor stood up, I'd slide under him, grab his leg, and try to knock him over. Instead, he'd run straight at me and knock me flat on my back every time. There was no sliding under, no clever moves, just me getting plowed over.

Times changed over the years, and so did our audience and some of our acts. We had to retire a few of our favorite bits based on feedback, and usually, it only took one complaint to WJW for something to get pulled from the show. For example, someone complained that the cap gun shooting during our basketball games was promoting violence, so we had to drop that. We also had to say goodbye to our sword trick in the magic show. Chuck and I never pushed back when WJW asked us to stop a particular act, but I have to say that some of those complaints seemed petty. It's remarkable how quickly things can shift from harmless to controversial. But we adapted, and it never stopped us from having fun and entertaining the crowd.

Red's

Whenever we were in the area, we always planned a stop at a nightclub called Red's in Akron. It was a huge, split-level venue that could hold several hundred people, and was the most popular spot in town. Local professional athletes were frequent visitors, and there were stories of Tom Hanks appearing at the club once when he was in town. (He spent a few summers in Cleveland early in his acting career.) The club's owner, known simply as Red, had a fondness for Chuck. Whenever we walked in, I'd say hello to Red, and in return I'd get a polite but perfunctory "How ya doing?" Chuck would get a huge hug and an enthusiastic, "Chuck! How are you doing, buddy? Great to see you!" Chuck had that knack for

I'll do most anything for charity. I wrestled Victor the bear multiple times. Does he look intimidated here? There was one rule when wrestling Victor, and I wasn't about to break it.

making people feel like old friends. We always had a great time at Red's. Red told the servers to ensure we never had an empty glass in our hands, so we learned to nurse our drinks to avoid passing out drunk on the floor. There were always great bands playing, and when we were there with the All-Stars and were ready to leave, Red would throw a case of beer on the bus for our ride home. On a couple of occasions, Red closed up the bar and let us stay to continue to the party.

Ghoulardifest

The ultimate public appearance extravaganza—a true highlight that held a special place in our hearts—was Ghoulardifest. For more than twenty years, that was the place for fans to celebrate our show and other favorite TV hosts. The inaugural Ghoulardifest took place in 1997, sparked by the desire to honor Ernie "Ghoulardi" Anderson following his death in February of that year. Traditionally, the event was held in October, shortly before Halloween. The guest list consistently featured Big Chuck, Bob "Hoolihan" Wells, and me, with a rotating cast of beloved characters from the show, including Art Lofredo, Mary Allen, Herb Thomas, Big Stash, Dick Goddard, and others. Local entertainers added flair to the mix, with bands, Jungle Bob, and new local movie hosts Janet Jay and James Harmon appearing in their on-air personas, The Mummy and The Monkey. The event also boasted a lineup of nationally known special guests, including Victoria Price, the daughter of legendary horror film actor Vincent Price; Forrest J. Ackerman, creator of *Famous Monsters of Filmland* magazine; and actors from the 1968 film *Night of the Living Dead.*

I'd never attended an event like this before. I was accustomed to making public appearances, but most lasted only a few hours. Ghoulardifest was a three-day festival. Sure, there were other guests, but I couldn't help but wonder who would want to see me, Hoolie, and Chuck for three whole days? I thought the show would be a disaster. Just before it opened, I walked by the entrance and saw people lined up down the driveway and around the corner. I was shocked! One year, my grandson was with me at the show, and afterward he said, "Papa, I can't believe how many people like you."

"Just because you think I'm old and unimportant," I said, "doesn't mean everyone feels that way."

At events like Ghoulardifest, we'd often sign hundreds of items in a single day. It's incredible what fans bring to be autographed—pictures, shirts, magazines, Frisbees, old *TV Guides*, and more. I sometimes wonder where they find this stuff! Some super fans even have promotional items I've never seen before. It's not unusual to spot a few fans wearing "certain ethnic sweaters."

Ghoulardifest started in 1997 as a way to gather fans and celebrate the late-night movie host tradition that started with Ernie Anderson and Chuck back in the 1960s and continued with our show. Here I am at a fest with Janet Jay and James Harmon, a.k.a. "The Mummy and The Monkey." *(C.R. Hendrix II)*

After forty-plus years of signing, I honestly couldn't even guess how many autographs I've signed. And Chuck was signing long before I started; if there is a world record for most autographs, he would be a contender. It was a huge disappointment for fans and me alike when the COVID-19 pandemic ended the convention.

We were constantly surrounded by crowds, which I am convinced is why Chuck and I rarely got sick. Exposure to so many people and their germs must have helped build up our immunity over time. We'd frequently encounter sick fans coughing and sneezing, and they'd often use the same hand they'd used to cover their mouth and nose to pat Chuck on the shoulder or me on the top of my head. Whenever I was the victim of a sneezy handshake, Chuck laughed, but he would stop when I rubbed my infected hand on him.

I've always been grateful for fans, and have enjoyed personal interactions with them at shows and other public appearances. They sometimes turn up asking me to autograph obscure memorabilia even I've never seen before. Check out those vintage issues of TV Showtime from the old Cleveland Press. Where do they find this stuff? *(C.R. Hendrix II)*

Learning Curve

I first wore an interruptible fold-back earpiece—an IFB—while hosting Cleveland's American Legion parade. This device enables on-camera talent to hear instructions from the program director while performing. As the parade started, the director began speaking to me through the IFB. I was startled and began turning my head, trying to figure out who was talking to me. I knew what the IFB was supposed to do, but I assumed the director would speak to me during the pauses in my lines—not right in the middle of my speaking. It's an art to speak at the same time someone is talking directly in your ear. It took me a while to get the hang of it, but

I'm pretty good at it now. The master of this was TV 8's on-air announcer, Bill Ward. He had the incredible ability to listen to someone deliver lines for the first time and repeat them flawlessly, whether for a commercial or another project.

Can't Sit in the Back

Whenever Chuck and I attended an awards show, we were expected to entertain; we couldn't just show up and blend in. One year, at the local Emmy awards, the prominent guest host was Jane Seymour, who was then starring in *Dr. Quinn, Medicine Woman*, a western-themed TV show. Chuck and I planned to attend as cowboys, and I visited a friend who owned a firing range to borrow some guns. I asked him to fill them with blanks—the biggest he had. When I arrived at the event fully armed, the security guard saw the guns and exclaimed, "Whoa, those are real—fantastic!" and let me right in, no questions asked. These days, I would have been tackled ten feet from the door and handcuffed. When Chuck and I were announced during the show, we leaped out of our seats and let loose with the guns. The noise was deafening and flames shot out of the barrels. I apologize to anyone who was there that night—I'm sure we gave you the scare of a lifetime.

Fuzzy Fun

The Woollybear Festival started in Birmingham, Ohio, in 1973, when Dick Goddard launched it as a small fundraiser for a local parent-teacher association. After a few years the festival was relocated to Vermilion, and there it grew into Ohio's largest one-day festival, attracting more than 100,000 attendees each year. Chuck and I were invited by Dick to participate in that first year's event, and we became regulars at the Woollybear Festival for decades. (And I'm still involved to this day.) After Chuck retired in 2020, whenever fans watching the parade asked me about him, I'd playfully tap the trunk of the car I was riding in and say, "He's tired; he's in here." Chuck and I spent decades together creating so much laughter and countless memories, and whenever he wasn't out with me, I could have just as easily tapped my head and heart and said the same thing: "He's in here."

At each year's Woollybear Festival, Chuck and I kicked things off with the preliminary Woollybear races. Next, we'd jump into the pet and kids' costume contests. Then, we'd assist Dick with announcements during the parade. After that, we wrapped up the final Woollybear races. It was a long day, from 8 a.m. to 7 p.m. Every year, I looked forward to seeing my Woollybear family, a core group of people who came to the festival for decades. They sat or stood in the same spot every year, and I've seen many of them grow from kids to parents.

In the early years, the event promoters held a post-parade picnic at their house, which we all attended. In the middle of one picnic, Clay Conroy, who you might also know as Woodrow the Woodsman, jumped out of his seat like his pants were on fire. My son, Dino, about three years old, had fallen into a cooler face-first while trying to get something to drink, and Woodrow leaped up and pulled him out. I credited Woodrow with saving my son's life.

One of the event organizers, Sam Coe, once noticed that I always stood, and asked why. I told him that when sitting, if your legs are six inches off the floor, they fall asleep. (I've been known to jump off a barstool and stagger around like I've had too many, but it's not because of the drinking; it's because my legs are asleep and I can't stand on them.) He made me a special chair to sit on, and I still use it every day at my house.

In 2024, I was honored to be asked to serve as the Grand Marshal of the parade—a distinct privilege to lead the festivities

With my good friend Neil Zurcher, of "One Tank Trips" fame, at the Woolly Bear Festival. Neil and I were tied for most Woollybear appearances when he passed away in 2025. *(Bonnie Zurcher)*

and deliver a speech. In 2024, Neil Zurcher and I were tied for attending the most Woollybear festivals, having participated every year since it began. Sadly, my dear friend passed away in January of 2025, and I won our contest for most shows attended. It's the little things that keep me motivated!

Go Speed Racer

We used to do personal appearances for the Lawson's convenience store chain. As part of their promotions for new-store openings, they would give away a go-kart. I suggested they give

Chuck and me one of those go-karts to drive in parades. I said it would be great advertising because not only would parade attendees see it, but pictures of Chuck and me driving it usually ran afterward in the local newspaper. Within a few weeks, we had a custom-painted go-kart.

It was fantastic for parades because it allowed me to maneuver from side to side to chat with people and stop for photos. On a few occasions when the go-kart was out of commission, fans seemed to miss it as much as if Chuck or I were missing.

I also used it to participate in a charity go-kart race around Public Square. Before the race, all the go-kart engines were tested and adjusted to ensure they performed equally, to eliminate unfair advantages. Despite this, I consistently came in second place to Browns offensive tackle Doug Dieken. Years later, I learned that after race officials checked and approved the karts, Doug's kart received some special last-minute adjustments back in the pits before the race.

Chuck and I kept the same go-kart for forty-five years, repainting it several times as we picked up new sponsors.

Always a Couple in Every Bunch

At one point, shortly after John Lennon was shot, the studio offered to provide bodyguards for our appearances, but Chuck and I declined. We loved meeting our fans, and, besides, if anyone wanted to harm me, I was easy to find at the jewelry store any day of the week. That said, there were two fan encounters I could've done without.

The first involved my hair. I had been nearly bald since my early twenties. Eventually I decided to get a hairpiece, inspired by the physical prowess act Chuck and I performed at All-Star basketball games. When I did handstands on Chuck's back for that act, my comb-over hung straight down and looked ridiculous. The hairpiece had its problems, too. At a softball game in Brook Park, a kid snatched the toupee right off my head. I had to chase him down to get it back. Fortunately, I was in great shape and could outrun the kid. The toupee got to be a pain in the ass, and after twenty years, I gave it up—and bald was my new look! My wife has seen me with and without hair, but she has never seen me without a mustache. I've only been clean-shaven once since I was an adult. Chuck and I made a bet on the show: If he lost, he would shave his head; if I lost, I would shave my mustache. Of course, there was no way Chuck would shave his head, so it was a foregone conclusion that I would lose.

The second involved my thumb. Chuck and I were hosting one of our annual Halloween parties at the Aurora Woodlands. While judging the costume contest, I stood in front of the stage and said, "Let's hear it for contestant number one," and pointed back with my thumb. To my horror, the contestant leaned forward and bit my thumb with such force that it sent a jolt of pain through me and drew blood. He clamped down and refused to let go, leaving me frantically trying to pry him off! My only option was to beat the guy on the head with my microphone. Chuck came rushing over, not knowing what was happening and thinking I had lost my mind. The drunk finally let go. This occurred in the late 1980s, when not much was known about AIDS. I spent several anxious weeks and made multiple trips to the clinic to ensure I hadn't been infected. To this day, I still have the scar as a reminder of that bizarre night.

I Wasn't Flirting with Your Wife

When the circus came to town, Chuck and I were ringmasters several times. Getting used to speaking with a mic in the large auditorium with an echo was a challenge. I'd talk, then pause to hear what I had just said echoing through the speakers—it was hard not to. After my first show, I asked my wife how I did. She turned to me and said, "You sounded like an idiot!" I always appreciate honesty.

I didn't realize there were two circuses—a red circus and a blue circus—that traveled and alternated each year. Each featured a unique lineup of acts and performers. I had become friends with some performers, including the clowns, many of whom were short like me. During the second year the circus was in town, I spotted one of the clowns and shouted, "Hiya, Mabel!" and blew her an innocent, friendly kiss. Out of nowhere, another clown came charging at me, obviously very upset.

"What the hell are you doing blowing kisses to my wife?"

"Your wife?" I didn't know Mabel was married!"

"That's not Mabel," he replied. The clowns wore heavy makeup, making it hard to tell who they really were.

Chuck, laughing the whole time, said, "That would've been the most bizarre fight I've ever seen!"

Not the only time I heard Chuck say that, either. One time Chuck and I were at a Muscular Dystrophy Association event, and the act before us featured a chimpanzee. Chimpanzees can grow over five feet tall and weigh more than a hundred pounds. One of the chimps was as tall as I was and stood beside me, glaring and grunting aggressively. I turned to Chuck and said, "I don't think he likes me." I reached over to grab the microphone stand—something I could defend myself with, just in case he attacked. Just then the chimp lunged at me and the trainer struggled to hold him back. Chuck, always quick to find the humor in any situation, grabbed me by the shirt collar as if he was holding *me* back from attacking the chimp. "That would've been the most bizarre fight I've ever seen!" he said again.

Family Friendly

Bob Hope was my childhood hero. He was known for his clean humor, and I always tried to emulate him. The comedy we used on the show remained consistently family-friendly, which suited me perfectly.

We were once asked to perform at a nightclub, and I explained that our show was not well-suited for an adults-only bar setting. I explained our edgiest humor was this joke: "Have you ever noticed how the trees down south lean toward Pittsburgh? That's because Pittsburgh sucks." However, the promoter insisted and asked how much we charged. I quoted a price ten times our usual rate, convinced that it would end the conversation, but he readily agreed. We arrived at the venue thirty minutes early and found that no one was there—absolutely no one. I wondered if we had shown up at the wrong place or time. Once I determined that we were in the right place at the right time, I wasn't sure whether to worry more about no one showing up or about the owner finding a reason not to pay us. I could not have been more surprised when the promoter came in before the show and paid us in full. That never happened.

Chuck and I were backstage, minutes before the show was set to open, and I began to hear the rumblings of a crowd. I poked my head out and saw the place was packed—wall to wall. Our first joke had me greeting the audience and saying that Chuck was a bit nervous and would be out shortly. I went on to praise him as a class act and a true professional, and that's when Chuck made his grand entrance, his shirt untucked and toilet paper stuck to his shoe. That bit always drew a show-opening laugh.

As the night went on, the cocktail waitress came by every ten minutes and gave Chuck and me a shot. Before long, we were several shots in. At one point during the show, I asked the audience, "Who's entertaining whom at this point?" Our act, which was supposed to last about two hours, ran until two in the morning. It turned out to be our only performance at a nightclub, but it was a hit.

Spend It; You Can't Take It With You

We recorded shows at various locations, including Cedar Point, Kalahari Waterpark, Las Vegas, and one of my favorite places, Walt Disney World. When I returned from my first trip, Disney sent a letter asking if I had enjoyed my stay because I hadn't spent much money, and they were worried I wasn't having a good time or that something was wrong. In a follow-up phone call, a Disney representative explained that Disney covered all my expenses while I was on their property, a detail I wasn't aware of. On subsequent trips, I was only too happy to take advantage of everything Disney had to offer. The joke among us was that we could visit with five dollars in our pocket and come home with the same five dollars, having done anything we wanted. Chuck was a homebody, and when shooting on location he enjoyed returning to his room in the evenings to relax and order a pizza. I preferred checking out different restaurants each night. Although Disney covered my expenses, a detailed report was printed at checkout. Chuck's expenses easily fit on one sheet of paper, while mine required the printer to be refilled.

On one Disney trip I asked a friend to come with me, and the food expenses ended up being more than when I visited alone. As I was checking out, the hotel agent said, "One moment, Mr. Rinaldi, you have expenses that need to be paid for."

I thought, *Oh boy, here it comes.* All the "free" perks will finally catch up to me. With hesitation, I asked, "How much?"

"A dollar ninety-eight," the clerk responded. The mini-bar

was not a covered expense, and I had taken a bag of peanuts one evening to snack on.

Disney liked having us shoot our show at their locations because of the free commercial time they got when it aired. We had an open invitation to shoot on location several times a year, all expenses paid. But Chuck liked to be home, so we didn't go as much as I would have liked.

We weren't often recognized at Disney because no one in Florida saw our show. But Disney must have picked up a busload of tourists from Cleveland one morning and dropped them off near where we were filming, because when the bus unloaded, people went nuts shouting, "Hey, Big Chuck and Lil' John!" Later that evening, a senior vice president from Disney invited Chuck, me, and a few other guests to dinner. When we showed up, the VP informed us that the restaurant was extraordinarily busy and it would be a few minutes before our table was ready. About that same time, a man walked by and said, "Big Chuck and Lil' John! What are you guys doing here?"

"We're shooting video for the show."

"Why are you waiting outside?"

"Our table isn't ready; they said it will be a while."

"What? How many are in your party?" the man asked.

The vice president answered, "Ten."

"Get these guys seated immediately," the guy said to the hostess. Apparently, he was some kind of secret shopper who reviewed restaurants and had enough cachet to get what he needed when he needed it.

SeaWorld in Aurora, Ohio, was another one of my favorite spots to shoot. I got to be a part of nearly every stage show when I was there. I once played a sheriff in a western show and participated in a fight scene. Let me tell you, breakaway bottles still hurt when you get hit in the head the wrong way! Even though I couldn't swim, I volunteered to take the top spot in the human pyramid

Filming a skit on location at Disney World in Orlando, Florida. Chuck jumped over the rail to get a shot, and within seconds, security descended on him like it was a terrorist raid. Disney loved having us film there, though—and I loved the all-expenses-paid trip!

for the ski show. I wasn't worried about drowning; I just wasn't sure how I was going to get to the top of the pyramid. One of the more muscular actors carried me like a toddler in his arms to get me into position, and then I maneuvered my way to the top by grabbing any useful body part of the skiing performers. My arm wrapped around one guy's neck and my foot on a girl's head. Somehow, I managed to make it up there. But then I thought, *How do I get down?* I still don't know how they did it, but the pyramid was dismantled one layer at a time, and I was dropped right at the shore—my feet didn't even get wet!

GIVING BACK

Fun for a Good Cause

Cleveland has been incredibly good to me, and I've always been eager to give back whenever possible. In addition to the All-Stars charity games and station-sponsored charity events that Chuck and I did together, I've volunteered at countless other charitable events on my own. I'd accept any invitation if I felt it was for a good cause, and I've bartended, served as a celebrity waiter, golfed, ridden horses, and participated in just about every imaginable situation. It's a simple philosophy, but I believe that what goes around comes around. If I can help raise money for a good cause just by showing up, that's good karma in my book.

At one celebrity bartender event, I told the crowd that if anyone put five dollars in the charity tip bowl, I'd balance a glass on my head. Soon enough, I had an entire tray of glasses stacked up there. But I lost my balance, and they all came crashing down. I then told everyone to put more money in, and I'd give it another try. That's when the bar manager came rushing over. "No, no, you won't!"

During a charity golf match, I made a bet with Bob Gain, the 250-pound offensive lineman for the Cleveland Browns: the loser had to wash the winner's back after a long, hot day of golfing. I lost, and when it came time to pay up, I wheeled an industrial-strength mop and bucket into the locker room, and said, "I think this should do it." Bob couldn't stop laughing, and fortunately he chose to wash his own back.

The guys I usually paired with for charity golf outings didn't take the game seriously, and neither did I; we just wanted to have a good time. We might even be seen hitting the ball polo-style while riding in the cart. I would even fill out the scorecard in advance. Not to cheat and win; I purposely filled out the card so we'd lose. I just didn't want to bother with the tedious chore of keeping score for every hole.

Cavs announcer Joe Tait, radio host Trapper Jack, and I were often invited to host the charity auction at the Cleveland Cavaliers' golf outing. Joe led the auction while Trapper and I worked the crowd to stir up bidding. We competed to determine who could secure the highest bids from our respective sides of the room. My strategy was to scan the room to see which side seemed to be drinking the most, and that's the side I'd target. I figured those guests might be looser with their wallets. We had a lot of fun raising money for a good cause.

I attended an auction at which Cavs owner Gordon Gund was in attendance. Gordon donated the use of a loge for an event at the Gund. Before the auction, I joked with him about me joining the basketball team. Gordon had lost his sight years before and was completely blind. He said, "By the way your voice hits my ear, I suspect you're about four feet tall. We don't need any more short guards!" The loge was one of the big items being auctioned that night. I convinced the food vendor to throw in free snacks to boost the bidding. Next, I got another business to throw in a TV. Then I added a clock from Rinaldi Jewelry—"So you'll know when it's time to go home," I told the crowd. Once that loge was auctioned off, I impulsively asked Gordon if he'd offer a second night at the same price for another bidder, and he agreed. We raised a substantial amount of money that night!

I was the emcee for a charity cancer auction featuring elaborately decorated Christmas trees donated by various organizations in the area, including the Cleveland Cavaliers and the

If I can help raise money for a good cause, that's good karma. Golf? Bartending? Horseback riding? I'll do it. Here I am serving tables for charity as a celebrity waiter.

Handicapped Workers of America. Throughout the night, I kept reminding everyone, "If you win a tree, you *must* pay tonight. No IOUs. Cash, check, or credit card—*no exceptions*." I must have said this twenty times. At charity auctions I usually bid on a few items myself expecting to get outbid. Sometimes, when people see my name on the bid list, they get a kick out of outbidding me. That night, though, I won the Handicapped Workers' tree. At the end of the night, I went to the table to pay—only to realize I didn't have my wallet. Sherry hadn't brought cash or her credit cards either. After lecturing everyone about paying on the spot all night, I could not pay for my tree! Shamefully, I promised them I'd return the next day with the money.

The tree was delivered to our house, but it was so big we couldn't get it through the front door. We had to ram it through the back patio door. It was covered in glitter, and when we shoved it through—boom!—glitter explosion! It looked like Christmas had detonated in our living room. To this day, I still find small pieces of glitter in random corners of the house.

Giddy Up

One time I participated in a charitable horse show and competition. I'm usually up for trying something new, especially for a good cause, so I naturally said yes when asked. But I told the organizers the only time I'd been on a horse was a couple of awkward pony rides when I was a kid. They reassured me I'd receive lessons before the event.

I showed up for my training, and without warning, my trainer's horse dropped to the ground and rolled over—almost trapping the trainer underneath. Shocked, I asked why the horse would do that. My trainer casually explained that it's not uncommon for horses to roll for all sorts of reasons: to scratch an itch, get comfy, or if they don't like being ridden for one reason or another. At my size, I immediately pictured myself being squashed into oblivion under my horse. It wouldn't be a glamorous way to go, being squashed next to the piles of horse shit lying about. My horse could tell I was inexperienced. Whenever I loosened control, he'd take the reins—literally—wandering where he wanted to or trotting back to the stable like he had a hot date.

On the day of the event, I was dressed and looked the part, but I was doing everything I could to avoid falling off—and thinking about what to do in case of a rollover. Local news media showed up with cameras rolling. As I rode by, one camera operator started moving his camera cords around, and my horse, evidently mistaking the cords for a snake, panicked. My instructor had told me that if I was ever in a situation where the horse became uncontrollable, I should grab the bridle on one side, and the horse would walk in circles. I did that, and after I got the horse under control, I talked to him for the rest of the event. "Easy now, you and I are friends. Let's have a fun day together."

A Match Made in . . . Cleveland

I've already shared the tale of stepping into the ring with boxing champion Mike Tyson. Not long after that event, I got another call: "John, how'd you like to battle in an exhibition match for charity at the Gund Arena in early February?"

This time I wouldn't have Chuck by my side, but I was still in great shape and ready to take on another world champ.

"You bet I would. Any time, any place."

And just like that, the match was set. I was scheduled to go toe-to-toe with Andre Agassi, one of the greatest tennis players of all time. As part of the National City Challenge Cup, we would be raising money for cystic fibrosis and other charities. Three matches were scheduled: an exhibition between tennis pros Andre Agassi and Pete Sampras, a game between the two pros and two lucky radio contest winners, and the final match between the two pros and two local celebrities.

There was just one small problem. I had never even held a tennis racket, let alone played a match. When I agreed, I figured, *How many people show up for a tennis match anyway?* The answer is 19,432. There wasn't an empty seat in sight at the Gund Arena. Afterward, I read that it was the largest indoor tennis gathering in Cleveland's history.

A couple of weeks before the match, I turned on the TV one afternoon to watch a game. Not to learn the rules, but to figure out what people wore. I was determined to at least look the part. The day of the match, I was escorted to a private locker room to get ready. I had my shorts, tube socks, and collared shirt . . . and that's when I realized I didn't have a racket! The promoters quickly solved the issue by providing me with one. The other local celebrity chosen for the match was Chris Mills, a six-foot, seven-inch forward for the Cleveland Cavaliers. He and I were dressed and ready, waiting to be announced for the celebrity match.

Chris casually asked, "Do you play tennis a lot?"

"Do I play tennis?" I replied, looking at my borrowed racket as if it were a fly swatter. "Never picked up a racket in my life before right now."

He stared at me wide-eyed. "You're kidding, right?"

"Nope. But how hard can it be?"

He suggested we hit a few balls in the hallway to warm up while we waited. I managed a few decent shots and was feeling pretty good about the whole thing. When the other two exhibition matches were done, Chris and I were ready to hit the court.

The loudspeaker echoed: "Ladies and gentlemen, please welcome power forward for the Cleveland Cavaliers, Chris Mills." A healthy round of applause followed as he ran onto the court. ". . . and now, half of the funniest duo on TV, from Fox 8, please welcome Lil' John Rinaldi!" The place erupted. I've had my fair share of applause, but nineteen thousand people cheering for me all at once was surreal and deafening. I was so overwhelmed; I don't even remember running out to the court.

The match-up was Sampras and me vs. Agassi and Mills. As I took my place next to my partner amid the thunderous applause, Sampras gave me a confused look. "Who the heck are you?" he asked.

"Ah, nobody," I shrugged.

Before the match, we had time to warm up, but I didn't realize we were supposed to volley. Agassi hit an easy shot past me, and I just watched it sail right by. Sampras looked at me like I'd lost my mind. "Why didn't you hit it back?" he asked.

"Oh, I'll get the next one," I assured him. The next ball came,

Pete Sampras and I partnered in a match against Andre Aggasi and Cleveland Cavaliers forward Chris Mills. I had never picked up a racket before. I thought, How hard could it be?

and I swung hard, not knowing how much power I was supposed to use. The ball rocketed right into section C—about twenty rows back—where it almost hit a lady in the head. Sampras was now looking very concerned. Still in warm-ups, I said to Agassi, "Hit one to me like you would in a real game." He told me to move over . . . a little more . . . a little more . . . until I was just about off the court. I saw the ball go up, heard the pop of his racket, and the next sound I heard was the ball slamming into the wall behind me. That ball would've knocked me out cold if it had hit me in the head. Once the warm-ups were over, I stepped over to the sidelines. NBA superstar LeBron James habitually used powdered chalk on his hands before a game and would throw some into the air to engage the crowd. So I grabbed a bag of chalk—and dusted my head with it. I might not be a tennis pro, but I can handle the comedy just fine.

With the match about to start, everyone was in position. I was in front, Sampras in the rear. Once we started play, with no clue how to play other than knowing the ball is supposed to be hit across the net, I started running and diving for balls, trying to hit everything at all costs. Sampras finally came up behind me and said, "John, do you mind if I tell you something?"

"Sure," I said, expecting compliments on my enthusiastic play and athletic prowess.

"You know, you have a partner, and he's pretty good. You can let some of those go by."

"Oh, sure thing, got it."

This was all for charity and fun, so no one was taking it too seriously—except maybe me. At one point, Agassi looked at me and said, "This one's for you, John." He then lobbed a serve so high into the air that it almost hit the ceiling of the arena. I tracked its flight and was sure it would go out of bounds, but that ball curved and landed right at my feet. That's how good these guys are.

Sampras looks at me, smiled and said, "You know, you can swing at those."

Agassi next looked at Sampras and said, "This one's for you." And proceeded to launch a rocket. I only had a split second to raise my racket, and by pure luck, I made contact. The ball hit so hard that it spun my racket around, smacking me hard in the head and stunning me for a moment. Once Agassi saw I was still standing—barely—he shouted, "I think I killed him!"

Although the match went into two tie-breakers it wasn't a big surprise my team lost! But the real mistake I made that night wasn't the match—it was not getting that borrowed racket signed by the two pros. Agassi and Sampras signed their own game-used rackets, which were sold for big money that night. I guess it was a swing and a miss on my part—several times on the court and once with that one-of-a-kind collector's item!

NOTHING VENTURED, NOTHING GAINED

Stick to What You Know

I love adventure and trying new things—businesses, hobbies, food, or anything in between. Sometimes I had no clue what I was getting into, and things didn't always go as planned, but I usually learned something in the process.

One of my business ventures that didn't work out as hoped was Celebrities restaurant and nightclub. Several other local celebrities were involved. Located on Rockside Road in Independence, the venue aimed to offer patrons a chance to see local celebrities during their visit. Giant metal stars bearing celebrities' names lined the entrance, reminiscent of the Hollywood Walk of Fame. The menu featured various food items, but one standout was the delicious prime rib, served in two sizes: the "Lil' John" at twelve ounces for $12.95 and the "Big Chuck" at fourteen ounces for $14.95.

Celebrities is where Chuck and I filmed a skit with WBA heavyweight champion James "Bonecrusher" Smith. In the skit, Chuck referees the match and announces, "No hitting below the belt," and the shot pans to me with my boxing shorts pulled up over my head. Celebrities closed not long after opening. I invested in the business a few months after it opened, and fortunately I avoided a significant financial loss because my investment check was never cashed.

Rinaldi's Pizza was another restaurant venture that fizzled. Along with a couple of partners, I opened a pizza shop near St. Edward High School in Lakewood, with ambitious plans to eventually franchise. We went to great lengths to get everything right—conducting taste tests to perfect our recipe and navigating city inspections to open on time. By the time we launched, we had perfected a delicious recipe.

However, I soon learned the perils of owning a cash-based business. I would call the store sometimes to check on the previous day's sales. Once I called when I knew that the night before, the accounting firm I used had ordered pizza for all their employees—so I was expecting a profitable day. I was told not only that sales were slow the day before, but that the accounting firm had ordered only one pizza. With thirty people working in the accounting office, that made no sense. I called the firm directly and learned they had ordered a dozen pizzas. That was my wake-up call—time to exit the pizza business.

I even once tried to get into the fine-fur business. I know it's not fashionable or even acceptable these days, but decades ago, owning a fur coat was an aspiration. My first mink was a second-hand find that I picked up on the cheap. It was an older coat with a few rough spots, but since I had to have it tailored to fit anyway, the seamstress cut those parts out. Let me tell you, if you're looking for warmth, mink does the trick.

Sherry got her first mink coat through a very savvy trade. I was working at the jewelry store when she walked in, draped in this beautiful fur, and, of course, I asked, "Where on earth did you get that?"

"I bought it", she said.

"With what?" I asked, knowing how expensive they were.

"Oh, I sold my engagement ring," she said, as casually as if she'd traded it for a cup of coffee.

You might think I'd be upset, but I wasn't. The ring was hers

Filming a skit with heavyweight champ James "Bonecrusher" Smith at Celebrities nightclub. The skit wound up being much better than my investment in the nightclub. *(Kevin Salyer)*

to do with as she pleased. So I just said, "Well, if that's what you wanted."

"I love it!" she beamed. "Besides, I can always get another diamond—we're in the diamond business, don't forget."

During my conversation with the fur distributor, I learned how lucrative that business was, and I couldn't resist asking how I could get in on it. "Easy," he said. "I'll send you ten furs on consignment to get you started." I immediately began picturing a new shop: I'd sell high-end furs on one side and jewelry on the other. "Great," I said. "Call me when you're ready to move forward." A few weeks passed and I didn't hear anything, so I called to check in. The woman who answered the phone said, "I'm sorry—Tony passed away." And just like that, I was out of the fur business before I got in.

Over time, I realized I should stick to the things I know best—jewelry and TV.

I'll Try Most Anything—Once

Not all my misadventures were business-related; some of the situations I found myself in were for the show. Chuck didn't really like participating in the thrill-seeking activities we did for the show. Despite our frequent visits to Cedar Point, I don't recall him ever riding a roller coaster. But I loved the thrill, so it worked out perfectly. I've done all kinds of crazy things for the show with only a couple of regrets.

I already mentioned that stressful bungee jump at the start of the book. (As you can see, I survived!) I found myself in another uncomfortable situation when Chuck and I agreed to scuba dive in a large tank for charity. We were to scoop up coins from the bottom. It seemed like a good idea, but there was just one problem—I still couldn't swim. We planned to get scuba-diving training, so I hoped for the best. However, when people of average height are learning in a pool, they can stand up if they have a problem, but this pool was deeper than I was tall, making me highly uncomfortable. Despite my initial struggles, I eventually got the hang of it. As it turned out, my smaller size made me more agile at maneuvering underwater than Chuck.

Chuck had several talented people he could've picked as his co-host, but I'm sure he made the right call with me. Sure, any one of the other talented people could've stepped in front of the camera, but no one would've been willing to keep our chaotic appearance schedule or pull off the ridiculous stunts I regularly did. I am also certain my winning smile, sparkling personality, and razor-sharp wit sealed the deal. Okay, that's enough—I'll show myself out.

All Shook Up—and Bruised Up

My headshot was featured in an American Federation of Television and Radio Artists brochure for a long time, but I never received any audition calls from it. Then, in 1995, someone called from Chicago and asked if I'd be interested in participating in an Elvis Presley–themed show. It was part of an event designed to promote Cleveland as a tourist destination, with the audience comprising travel agents from across the country. The event was scheduled for a Sunday evening, the same time as my regular paid hosting gig at Hilarities comedy club in Cleveland. I didn't want to give up Hilarities, so I asked the caller how much I'd be paid for the Elvis show. Surprisingly, it was ten times what I made at Hilarities. I didn't think twice. My friend, Nick, the owner of Hilarities, was kind enough to give me the night off.

The show featured one hundred Elvis impersonators performing various acts. There was a tall Elvis, a skinny Elvis, a fat Elvis . . . and you can guess which Elvis I was. Before the show, they asked if I would ride a bicycle as part of my act for an additional $250, to which I agreed. I was to ride a bike styled like a Harley-Davidson motorcycle onto the stage, dismount, and strike a pose. At the same time, a group of Elvises would rappel down from the ceiling.

Just as I was about to ride out onto the stage, the event coordinator stepped in front of me to have a look—she hadn't been to rehearsals and didn't know anything about the highly choreographed show. Her unexpected move caused me to swerve and miss my mark on stage. I rode directly into the path of the rappelling Elvises, was knocked off my bike, and fell into the orchestra

That's me on the bike, dressed as Elvis—like everyone else in the show. (These are just a few of the Elvises—there were dozens!) Rehearsal went well, but the actual performance was a wreck—at least for me.

pit. My Elvis wig and glasses went flying, and the bike landed on me and then bounced into the lap of an audience member. Despite the chaos, I quickly gathered myself and returned to the stage to strike the pose as initially planned. At the time, I thought I was OK, but the next morning, I felt like I had been run over by a garbage truck.

Still Like Nails on a Chalkboard

In the late 1990s, Chuck and I were invited to sing on an upcoming album by polka legend Frankie Yankovic. Steve Popovich, the well-known record producer and founder of Cleveland International Records, was producing the project. It was a great opportunity . . . except I still couldn't sing. I repeatedly told Steve this, but he insisted that both Chuck and I be featured. We would be singing along to a prerecorded track, so the day we arrived at the recording studio, it was just Chuck, me, and the sound crew. After a few attempts, Steve called out, "Hey John, you weren't kidding when you said you can't sing."

"I told you that!"

After some discussion, they decided to turn my part into *sprechstimme*—a German term for "speech voice," basically speaking with a bit of musical tone. The album went on to be nominated for a Grammy. If it had won, that would've been incredible—an Italian who can't sing winning a Grammy! I wouldn't have minded adding a Grammy award alongside my collection of Emmys. For those who would like to give it a listen, the song is titled "My Melody of Love."

I've often embraced the phrase "Fake it till you make it." A prime example is when my friend Dave called me to fill in for the guitarist in his band who was sick.

"I don't know how to play the guitar," I told him.

"You don't need to," he replied. "Just stand up there and pretend."

That was good enough for me. Despite the guitar not even being plugged into the amp, I must have delivered a fantastic air guitar performance because my aunt, who had known me my entire life, was at the event and told me afterward, "I didn't know you could play the guitar."

Losing Altitude

I've been in hot-air balloons three times, and each experience was progressively worse. The first time, Chuck and I were supposed to ride near Lake Erie off Edgewater. The winds were howling at twenty miles per hour, perfect for flying a kite but not for hot-air balloons. The promoters were eager to get us in the air, but the aeronaut (what the pilot of a hot-air balloon is called—you can look that up; it's true), with all the seriousness of a man who has seen a few balloons crash, said, "We're balloonists, not daredevils" and promptly canceled the launch.

The next time, Chuck and I were in Mansfield. The plan was to go up only about a hundred feet and stay tethered to the ground, but the tether snapped and we launched unexpectedly. Suddenly, Chuck and I were up in the basket, alone, with the balloon racing through the air, while a crowd came running after us, trying to catch the tether line. Sounds like a show skit. Eventually, several spectators grabbed the tether line and stopped us before we crashed into an oncoming fence.

The third and final time, I was with Sherry and another couple south of Cleveland in a very rural area. The weather was calm and quiet, and we got off the ground OK. From above we could see squirrels playing in the trees and small lakes stretched out below. If you've never taken a ride in a balloon, it's a unique experience to see the world from a different point of view. But then came two words you don't want to hear from your surgeon or your accountant—or your hot-air balloon pilot: "Uh oh!" He announced, "I've got to get this thing on the ground right now." Somewhere over Kent, the pilot spotted a place to land, and we hit hard. The basket tipped over, and I scrambled to climb out. "Get back in," the captain said. "I need the weight or we're going to float away!" Everyone else was smashed into the basket like sardines. We had landed in someone's garden. A woman came out of the house and in true *Green Acres* fashion, said, "Hey Pa, we got a hot-air balloon in the garden!" Then, after seeing me, she excitedly added, "Pa, Lil' John landed in our garden!" Our hosts then called their kids and friends: "Come on over—Lil' John is in our garden!" When we finally got ready to leave, we left with a dozen bags of fresh produce. All in all, not a bad end to the day.

NOT SHORT—FUN SIZE

I'm Just Me

When I think about my size, and it's not to make a joke, it's usually to figure out how to use it to my advantage. I mean, I'm Lil' John after all! But like everything else in my life, I've chosen to find humor in it.

Once, while vacationing, I was getting out of a hot tub just as this 6′4″ and 225-pound guy was getting in. I said, "Hey buddy, I wouldn't get in there if I were you."

Confused, he asked, "Why not?"

"I was your size when I got in."

There have been only a couple of times when I've felt genuinely frustrated by my height—both were at Cedar Point. My high school senior class went to Cedar Point, and instead of the anticipated day of fun, it turned out to be a day of frustration. On the water ride, it was typical for the usually taller boy to sit behind the girl, but my height meant I had to sit in front of my date. As we moved on to the roller coasters, I was told by the staff checking guests' height that I couldn't ride. Ironically, I could have driven a car to the amusement park, but was not allowed on many rides. I spent most of the day holding the girls' purses.

Two decades later, I was back at Cedar Point shooting for our show. The park always provided a tour guide to help Chuck and me navigate the long lines for the rides. As I prepared to get on one of the rides, I spotted that all-too-familiar look on the height checker's face. I dashed behind our photographer and asked him to stand in front of me to block her view. Unfortunately, it was too late. By that point in my life, I had ridden every coaster in the park many times without a hitch. Despite my pleas and the fact that we were filming for the TV show, she was adamant that I couldn't ride. Eventually, a senior vice president was called, and he explained to her that the rule was meant to keep children who couldn't safely hold on from riding. I was allowed to ride.

Got My Back

I've never been one to get upset about comments or actions about my height from others, even when I know it is malicious. However, that didn't always apply to my friends. One night in Geneva, Ohio, I was with a group of buddies waiting to get into a bar. As people entered, their hands were stamped with a specific color based on whether they were under or over the legal drinking age. Instead of stamping my hand, the bouncer got cute and smacked my forehead with the stamp. Before I could even respond, my friend leaped over me and lit that bouncer up. The police showed up, and although they usually side with the bouncer, after hearing what happened they allowed us to leave without further action.

The Ground Round, a restaurant, was famous for letting patrons throw empty peanut shells on the floor after eating the peanuts. A guy sitting at the bar thought it would be funny to toss peanuts at me. After the third one, I calmly approached him and said, "Okay, it was funny the first couple of times, pal, but enough with the peanuts." I thought that would settle things. However, as he and his friend got up to leave, he smashed a bowl of peanuts over my head. Big mistake! My good friend Mickey, just out of the armed services, punched this guy so hard that he flew over a table and landed on the next one over. It looked just like something out of an old western movie. While I am not an advocate of violence, it felt good knowing my friends had my back.

Snow Thank You

To quote the chorus from my friend Michael Stanley's song "My Town," I love Cleveland and everything about it. Except the snow. Now, before any snow lovers get upset with me, let me explain. I've done my best to embrace the cold weather. I've been ice skating, sled riding, skiing, and ice fishing, but none of them erase the trauma of one childhood memory. Today, winters in Cleveland seem to be milder than when I was a kid. While the city still gets its fair share of snow, it usually melts in just a few days. Back in the day, snow could start piling up as early as November, and those same mounds would still be around in March. The more it snowed, the bigger the piles got, and we kids had a great time climbing those towering mounds and walking across the tops. I was perched atop one of those mountainous piles while waiting for the bus on one of my return grocery trips. One hand was loaded with heavy grocery bags; the other clutched the exact change for the fare. As the bus approached, I shifted my feet, preparing to step from the snow pile onto the bus. Instead, my right leg sank straight into the snow while my left leg shot out in front of me like a catapult. I tried to pull myself out, but with every attempt to free myself I only fell deeper.

The bus door swung open, and Bill, the driver, whom I knew, was greeted by me, the live snow sculpture! He burst into laughter. I was not amused in the slightest. Bill got out to help. He told me to drop the groceries and grab his hand. I flatly refused. There was no way I was going to lose those bags and have to explain to my

I love a good thrill. There were a few times when a trip to the amusement park was less amusing, though.

mother what happened. Meanwhile, passengers began wondering why the bus wasn't moving and looked out the windows to see what was wrong. I could hear the laughter inside the bus and felt my growing embarrassment and intense frustration.

Bill climbed back in and backed the bus up a few feet to give himself more room to work. With all his strength, he finally lifted me out, groceries and all. I could hear applause from inside the bus, which only added to my mortification. I got on the bus and tried to move to a seat as inconspicuously as possible. Although the loud laughter had died, chuckles and murmurs still floated around me. I don't embarrass easily, but that day I would have welcomed the earth to open and swallow me up. It was one of those childhood moments that stick with you. And that is why I hate winter!

Here We Go Again

Quoting another song, this time "Here We Go Again," the Ray Charles tune we played frequently on the show. Fast-forward about thirty years. I had been invited by my friend to hunt at the Ravenna Arsenal. The night before, there was significant snowfall and brutally cold temperatures, and I called him to cancel. He insisted I come, explaining how many strings he had to pull to get me in. Not wanting to disappoint him, I agreed. It was 5 a.m. and pitch black when I arrived at the club. Running late, I took a shortcut across a field to get to the meeting spot. Unfortunately, I stepped into a deep ditch filled with snow and sank right up to my chest. My legs were twisted beneath me and I was stuck. I couldn't fire my shotgun to signal for help because for safety reasons I never loaded my gun before reaching the hunting site, and my ammo was now buried under the snow below me. After several minutes of struggling, I began to get cold and panicked with thoughts of freezing to death before anyone could find me. Just then, a fellow hunter, arriving later than I did, saw me and pulled me out. Add that to my Why I Hate Winter list.

Speaking of shotguns, I recall purchasing my first one. Because of my height, the sporting goods store had to shorten the stock to fit me properly. They said that would take a couple of days. I later got a call at the jewelry store, and the guy on the other end said, "Mr. Rinaldi, I'm adjusting your shotgun. Based on the measurements I have, you'd have to be a midget to use this thing." (This was before the term had its current negative connotations.)

"I am," I replied.

"Oh, I'm terribly sorry, Mr. Rinaldi. I'll have it done tomorrow, sir."

I don't hunt anymore. For some reason, deer don't seem to have the decency to show up at a reasonable hour, like after lunch, and

I'm not the type anymore to roll out of bed at 5 a.m. to freeze in the woods in a tree stand. In retrospect, I never had much luck deer hunting anyway—maybe it had something to do with the fact that I'd head into the woods with my headphones on, a cigar in my mouth, and a noisy little portable heater at my feet.

Fashion Icon, Kids Edition

I've always worn nice suits, which were necessary for my work at the jewelry store. Occasionally, men would ask where I got my suit and how much it cost, and I would happily share the details. More than a few times, when I saw them again they would say, "I went to get that same suit, but it wasn't anywhere near the price you paid."

"Oh, were you looking at the boys' size 18? I'm not sure about the cost of the adult-sized suits."

I shopped for clothes in the young men's section for most of my adult life, but when I got older and lost the slim build of my youth, I started shopping in the men's section. From that point, most of my clothes required alterations. My tailor, Audrey—now in her eighties—has for the past forty years worked on nearly every article of clothing I've owned. Except for socks and shoes, every piece of clothing I buy has to be altered, including my boxers, because they are too long. The upside of having a tailor is that I can buy clothes of any size. Sometimes, when I find something I like but it's only available in the wrong size, I buy it anyway. Even though Audrey is a master at making garments look like they were made just for me, she often asks, "John, did you have to buy a double X? Couldn't you find something reasonably close to your size?"

It's Not the Size that Counts

I've adapted to my height. When I need to reach for something out of my grasp, I instinctively find something to step on. If I need the salt shaker, I'll pull it closer with a spoon or a knife—these actions have become second nature. Driving, however, is slightly more complicated. I've always had to have blocks attached to the pedals so I can reach them. Decades ago, removing those blocks was tedious, so they stayed permanently attached, making it challenging for anyone of average height to drive my car. When Sherry or the kids got behind the wheel, the pedals would push their legs and knees into an awkward position. When Sherry was pregnant, she had to drive with her knees pressed against her stomach! Fortunately, newer pedal designs can be easily moved aside, allowing someone of normal height to drive comfortably.

A few years back, my exceptionally tall friend Jim, an amateur photographer, invited me to a photo shoot at Myakka River State Park in Florida, a hot spot for alligator sightings. The trek was about two miles from the parking lot to the alligator hangout. On our way, Jim slowed his walking pace to accommodate my short stride. Once there, Jim snapped pictures and I enjoyed the scenery. The park has a system: visitors check in and receive a pass, which they must return so the rangers know they didn't become a gator snack during their visit. After watching the alligators for a while, I told Jim, "Stay as long as you want. I'll get a head start so I don't slow you down on the walk back." It was hot, and I figured I'd get back to the car and relax while waiting for Jim. As soon as I reached the parking lot, I looked behind me and saw Jim strolling out of the woods like he'd been right behind me the entire time.

"I thought you were going to stay a while," I said with surprise.

"I did. I stayed forty-five minutes after you left."

I once participated in a charity stair climb for cystic fibrosis at

Erieview Tower—forty floors. For weeks, I trained by taking the stairs whenever I had the chance, convinced I'd be in top form by the big day. When the day came, as chairman of the event I was honored to start the event by being the first to head up the stairs. I was feeling pretty confident. But about ten floors in, I heard what sounded like a stampede and then the firefighters blew by me like I was standing still, taking four steps at a time. I tried doubling my steps, too, but damn near broke my neck, so I decided I'd stick to one step at a time. Then came another kick in the pants: the visually impaired participants were passing me by, too. I chugged along and finished within a reasonable time frame for my age group. Sometimes, it's not about speed; it's about crossing the finish line with no broken bones.

A LITTLE TROUBLE HERE AND THERE

Automatic Door Locks

I was up early on New Year's Day to meet friends for a day of sledding. Before leaving my apartment, I changed into old clothes and swapped my nice watch for an old Timex with a Mickey Mouse logo. While driving on Ansel Road, not far from home, I pulled up to a stoplight and saw a guy standing at the corner bus stop. We nodded to each other, a casual Happy New Year greeting. Then, before I could process what was happening, he was suddenly in the car holding a gun to my head. This was before automatic door locks were standard on cars, and because of my height I had a hard time reaching across the seat to lock the passenger-side door, so it was usually unlocked.

At first, I thought he was nervous and couldn't hold the gun steady, but later realized it wasn't the weapon shaking; it was me trembling with fear. He told me to drive to a secluded side street, and there he demanded all my cash. I handed over the little money I had on me, but he insisted I was hiding more. He started rummaging through the car and then began badgering me again for more money. He demanded my watch, but after looking it over, he sneered, "You can keep that piece of shit." Realizing finally that I didn't have anything else of value, he exited the car and started walking away. It took me a moment to process what had happened, but within seconds, I went into a rage. I slammed the car into drive and went after him, but he slipped away between some houses. This was probably for the best, because I wasn't thinking straight at that moment, and I'm not sure what would have happened had I caught up with him.

After the incident, I went to the police station to report it. When they asked me to describe the guy, I realized I had no idea what he looked like, even though he'd been just inches from my face. My description was so vague that it could fit any male in the city. They asked about the gun, and all I could say was, "It was a gun and it was pointed at my head."

When I bought my next car, the first thing I asked was, "Does it have automatic locks?"

They Weren't Window Shopping

While I was working at Cowell & Hubbard, one day one of the salesmen told me a couple had just stolen a ring from the store. Even though there were usually police officers on duty in the mall, none were in sight, so I followed the couple out to the parking lot. "Hey you! Give me that ring back." I said. "If you give it back, there won't be any trouble." For a second, I thought I had made a big mistake as the guy reached into his pants—I presumed for a gun. But to my relief, he pulled out the ring and handed it back. Proudly, I went to tell the store manager about my quick-thinking heroics. Instead of praising me, as I expected, the manager looked at me and said, "You risked your life for a ring? John, we have insurance for that kind of thing." I was sent home for the rest of the day without pay. Lesson learned!

Months later, in a similar incident, I flagged down a mall cop. The cop stopped the thief and asked about the ring, but the guy didn't say a word. After a second warning that he'd be arrested if he didn't answer, the guy punched the cop in the face, and a fight ensued. Other cops rushed over. At one point, the cop's gun fell out of its holster, and my heart was pounding as I stood just feet away and watched.

After the cops had the guy in handcuffs, they took him to the on-site security office and questioned him about the ring, but still silence. They searched him and found the ring in his pants. The case went to court, and, ironically, I was seated next to a cop from Higbee's department store who was there for the brother of my thief, who was also in court on theft charges. The defendant in our case pleaded not guilty, and his lawyer offered a wild excuse. He claimed the defendant thought he was supposed to go to a kiosk in the middle of the mall to pay for the ring.

When I heard this, I involuntarily blurted out, "That's not true; he didn't even have any money on him when they searched him!"

The judge glared at me, "One more word, and I'll hold you in contempt." Then the judge asked the defendant, "Is that true? Were you going to pay for the ring at the kiosk?" The guy nodded. To my astonishment, the judge announced, "The ring was returned; this case is dismissed." And somehow, the fact that the guy had punched a cop in the face never even came up!

Gone in Sixty Seconds

One Christmas Eve, a customer called the store, saying he didn't have time to pick up his wife's gift before closing and asked if I could drop it off at his business. I said sure; his place was on our way home anyway. My car had been acting up and needed a push-start to get it running, so when Sherry and I arrived at the customer's location I didn't want to turn the engine off. But I also didn't want to leave Sherry alone in the car since I knew I would be inside longer than just a minute or two and it wasn't a neighborhood where you want to leave your wife in the car. So we left the motor running, locked the car doors, and went inside with the package.

While I was talking with the customer, Sherry glanced at a security monitor in the office. "John, there's a guy hanging around the car." I was busy talking and didn't pay much attention. A few seconds later, she said, in a panicked tone, "John! He just smashed the window, and he's stealing our car!" My customer bolted outside, reached through the broken car window, and grabbed the driver by the neck. The car pulled away, and he was half in and half out, being dragged down East 27th Street like an action hero in a movie. Eventually, he let go, and we watched the car drive out of sight.

I called 911.

"911, what's your emergency?"

"Someone just stole my car! They're driving down 27th—"

"Name please?"

"The car's a green Oldsmobile—"

"Name, please?"

"John Rinaldi. Anyway, it's a green Oldsmo—"

"Address please?"

The police arrived within minutes, and they soon found the car near East 77th and St. Clair Avenue. An officer asked if I wanted to come to the scene to retrieve my vehicle. When we arrived, my Oldsmobile was up on blocks, the wheels gone and the radio ripped out.

The police knocked on the door of the nearby house. Sherry and I had done some Christmas shopping earlier and had purchased bags of candy, bottles of liquor, and blankets. As we entered the home with the police, many of the items we had purchased were there. Four small kids were huddled in the living room with only the oven on for heat. Seeing those kids living in those conditions, I asked the officer if we could leave the candy and blankets for them. He shook his head no. "We can't. It will send the wrong message—that crime pays." Had it been my decision, I would have left the stuff, but I understood and didn't argue.

Meanwhile, back at my customer's business, Sherry was understandably upset. Not only did these guys have my car keys, but they also had the keys to our house. My generous customer not only offered us his prized MG to drive home, since we had no car, he also said he would send one of his guys to our house to install new locks. I just had to pick up the new locks on the way home. I stopped by a local department store that was open late. Remember, it's Christmas Eve, and the place is packed with people, all in a last-minute panic to buy. (Crowded stores on Christmas Eve always puzzled me. It's not as if Christmas sneaks up on anyone.) When I got to the register to check out, I held up the locks and asked the cashier, "So, do you think my wife will like these for Christmas?"

Later, in court, the thief appeared with his four younger siblings and pleaded not guilty. He explained to the judge that if he went to jail, the kids would end up in foster care because he was the only one around to take care of them. The judge asked me, "Mr. Rinaldi, what do you think we should do?"

"Well, your Honor, I think you ought to get him a job at Sears Auto Center," I said. The judge looked confused, so I explained, "When my car was stolen, it was eighteen degrees out, and he stripped four tires by hand, no pneumatic tools, and removed the stereo—all in fifteen minutes! Sears takes four hours just to put four tires on my car!" The judge laughed and let the guy off without jail time.

About a year after I opened my own store on East 9th Street, I was on my way back after taping the show at the TV station. I was alarmed to see police cars surrounding the store. A customer had come in and asked to see a ring, then handed it back, and left along with his friend. My employee quickly realized the ring was a nearly identical fake. Without hesitation, he ran after the two men, but they split up, forcing him to chase just one. Sherry quickly called the police, and since we were downtown, they showed up almost immediately. Sherry told them our guy had left to chase the thieves, and since the cops knew my employee, it didn't take long for them to track him down along with the crook. They arrested the guy, only to discover he didn't have the ring—his partner, the one who had run the other way, did. With no evidence, they had to let him go.

About a month later, I was summoned to court for a discrimination lawsuit. The claim was that our employee had targeted and chased the first minority person he saw. Thankfully, my insurance included legal support. The opposing lawyer was a cousin of the two suspects and was pushing hard for a bogus settlement. My insurance company was ready to settle, offering $10,000 to resolve the nuisance case, but I refused. I argued that if I settled, it would send the wrong message to thieves that they could rob me and walk away with a big payday. After three days of testimony, the judge dismissed the case.

False Alarm

While Sherry, one of my salesmen, his young son, and I watched a holiday parade pass by our store on East 9th Street, police cars raced toward us. They weaved through the parade floats and the crowd as if responding to a murder scene. They screeched to a halt in front of my store and jumped out with shotguns, ready for action.

"John, have you been robbed?" they yelled as they rushed into the store.

"Robbed? What are you talking about?"

My salesman's son had wandered behind the counter and pressed the alarm button, unknowingly triggering a full SWAT-style response. Even though it became clear we weren't in any danger, the officers made us all sit silently while they carefully searched the store, just to ensure it wasn't a hostage situation.

The Cleveland SWAT team used to come by the store at Christmas to use costumes I borrowed from the show for their annual visit to Rainbow Babies and Children's Hospital. These big, burly guys would dress up as Santa Claus, clowns, and reindeer to cheer up sick kids, and Sherry would help them get ready, doing their makeup in the jewelry store's back room. These were big, tough guys carrying guns. I always prayed that if I was going to get robbed, let it happen on the day I've got a whole armed commando team in the back room! What always struck me was seeing these guys, who looked like they could rip apart a brick wall with their bare hands, get choked up before they left to visit these sick kids.

More Trouble in Solon

Most of these incidents happened downtown, but when I eventually relocated the store to suburban Solon, that didn't exempt us from crime. One time, a man came into the store with a heartwarming tale—he wanted to get a gift for someone who had been like a father to him. I showed him a nice $2,000 bracelet, but when I handed it to him, he ran out the door with it. I began chasing him, but he was faster than me, and I lost him completely when he jumped into a waiting car. Meanwhile, back at the store, the employees had already called the police, who were speeding over to help—and drove right past the guy's car on the way. I later learned the guy hit five jewelry stores that day.

Security cameras at the bowling alley behind my store captured footage of the getaway car. When the police reviewed the video, they could not read the license plate but did notice the car was missing a hubcap. Later, a sharp-eyed cop on patrol spotted a white vehicle matching the getaway car's description and recalled that the APB had mentioned the missing hubcap. That was enough to crack the case. The police blocked off the street, and then noticed several people coming and going from one house. They were sure it was a drug house. They didn't have a search warrant, but when they walked up to the house, the door was wide open and an older gentleman sitting inside waved them in without realizing they were police officers. A younger guy bolted up the stairs, and the older guy, who was the kid's father, told the officers with a sigh, "Go get that rotten son of a bitch—he hasn't paid rent in months!"

The window of my downtown jewelry store was broken twenty-seven times. It got smashed so often that I kept a wooden insert on hand to put up each time until it could be repaired. I used to tease the guy who fixed the window by saying, "Business must be slow this week," implying he'd broken it. Someone threw a chunk of concrete through the door once, hitting a showcase in the middle of the store. It must have been eight pounds of concrete. I told the cops, "If you find him, sign him up for the Indians—he's got a hell of an arm."

PART-TIME ELF

Ho Ho Hold It, I'm Out

Ralph was a local film editor who had a genuine passion for playing Santa Claus unlike anyone I've ever met. He filled that role in several skits for *The Big Chuck & Lil' John Show*, fully embodying the character in spirit and appearance. He was so authentic that he would cheerfully answer the phone with a hearty "North Pole!" Every holiday season for several years, Ralph arranged surprise visits to children's homes, arriving as Santa himself. Since I wasn't married yet and had plenty of free time, he asked me to tag along as his elf, and I happily agreed.

Some of the children we visited were the kids of his friends or acquaintances, but many were children Ralph had never met. I never asked for the details, but somehow he connected with parents of underprivileged families who could use a little extra holiday cheer. The visits were completely free; it was just our way of giving something back.

Ralph coordinated the visits with the parents, but with multiple stops per night, and visits varying in length, he kept our arrival times flexible. On a typical visit we would arrive at the house and greet the parents, and then I would quietly enter their child's bedroom and gently ring a little bell to wake them up. I would carry the child downstairs to meet Santa and receive gifts (which their parents had purchased). It all went well for several years, until it didn't.

Have you ever been in a situation where your sixth sense told you something wasn't right? Very late one evening, Ralph and I arrived at one of our scheduled stops. The house was completely dark, inside and out, and I asked Ralph if he was sure this was the right place. He assured me it was. As we approached the door, there were still no signs of life. Ralph opened the door and stepped inside, and I followed, still unsure. He told me where the child's bedroom was, and off I went. I entered the bedroom quietly, only to be confronted by an angry and fully awake adult man sitting in bed, looking straight at me. "You son of a bitch, what are you doing in my house?"

I began backpedaling, "Oh, I'm sorry. I think there has been a mistake."

"You're damn right; you've made a big mistake." I was sure the guy was going to reach under the bed, pull out a shotgun, and blow my head off. I began envisioning the headline in the morning paper: "Local TV Celebrity Lil' John Rinaldi Shot Dead Breaking Into Home Dressed as Elf."

Despite the yelling and the sound of kids now crying in the other room, I somehow managed to calm him down just long enough to allow me to turn around and leave. Ralph and I figured the wife must not have told her husband we were coming, and instead of greeting us at the door had fallen asleep.

I should have called it quits after that, but it took one more incident to convince me. On another very late evening, we drove past a house with a big bay window. We could see a couple in the middle of a heated argument. Ralph slowed down, stopped, and got out of the car. He was headed straight for the front door.

"Hey, what are you doing? I don't think that's a good idea," I warned.

"It'll be all right; Santa can settle any argument," Ralph said.

I stupidly followed him toward the house, with the utmost reservations. "I'm not sure about this," I said. "They look furious."

As we walked up to the door, Ralph was in full swing, Ho, Ho, Ho-ing and shouting, "Merry Christmas!" with all the festive cheer he could muster. Ralph was still several steps from the door when

Ralph Gertz was a terrific Santa—the real deal. His planning, though, was kind of . . . loose. The kid in this photo was happy to see us, but a later visit didn't go so well—leading to my abrupt retirement as Ralph's elf.

the guy opened it, and with eyes wild and glazed said, "You two assholes better get the hell out of here before I beat you to death." As big of a heart as Ralph had for bringing joy to the families and children he visited, and as much as I loved being part of it, that was my last sleigh ride with Ralph.

Wrong House

Being at the wrong house seems to be a recurring theme for me. Sherry and I were attending a friend's wedding reception at a restaurant, and the plan was for guests to be driven on a bus back to the bride and groom's house for an after-party. After getting off the bus, we went to our car parked down the street to grab the wedding present we had for the couple. When we returned, the bus had left and all the guests were gone. We didn't remember exactly which house the party was at, so naturally we chose the house with all the lights on, and strolled in through the open side door. I spotted a woman at the sink doing dishes, and my first thought was, "Oh great, they've hired help for the party." But as we walked further in, I noticed a guy lounging on the couch in shorts, with kids scattered across the floor—this definitely wasn't the after-party.

Instead of freaking out, the guy looked up at us like we were old friends and said, "Hey, Lil' John, what are you doing here?" I quickly explained that we were headed to a wedding party and accidentally picked the wrong house. He smiled. "No worries, come on in, have a drink." I politely declined, and as we quickly left I said, "You should really lock your doors—you never know who might wander in."

Sherry and I were invited to a big Christmas party at the home of a Fox8 executive. It was already dark and snowing heavily on the ride over, making it difficult to read the house addresses. As we turned onto the street, one house was lit up, and it was clear that a huge Christmas party was going on. As soon as we walked in, I realized no one else there was from the station. Of course, I got the same courteous greeting: "Hey, Lil' John, what are you doing here?" We later learned that Dick Goddard and Robin Swoboda had made the same wrong-house mistake that night.

Another time, I was running late to a wedding reception being held at a party center. While dinner was already in progress, I rushed in and hastily threw my gift envelope in the collection box. As I looked around, I realized there wasn't anyone I recognized. The policeman at the door asked who I was there for, then informed me I was at the wrong wedding. I said, "Okay, but I have a problem—I already put my envelope in the wedding box." He was kind enough to fish it out for me.

I have tried to be more careful, but if I ever show up in your living room unannounced and uninvited, don't be alarmed—I've just made a mistake and mean no harm!

Santa, an Elf, and . . . a Dog?

Although my Santa visits with Ralph ended, that didn't end my role as a Christmas elf. My friends Dave and George had access to a full-body dog costume through their workplace, and I suggested we spread holiday cheer, with a twist. We'd visit families dressed as Santa, an elf, and a giant dog. We partnered with various local organizations to identify families who couldn't afford a Santa visit and needed extra holiday joy. For nearly twenty-five years, we dedicated ourselves to this cause, visiting all kinds of neighborhoods, and no matter the location, everyone was glad to see Santa.

Whenever we were out and I was driving, I had a mental cue for when to hit the gas and take off to our next stop—because we had a schedule to keep. I would listen for four car doors to shut. Door one was me getting into the driver's side, door two was Dave getting into the front passenger seat, door three was George putting the big dog head from his costume in the back seat, and door four was George getting into the other side of the back seat. One time, I heard the four doors shut and was about to take off when I heard a muffled cry from Dave pleading, "No, wait, wait, don't go yet!" He had slipped on some ice while trying to get in, the door had shut, and he had fallen partly under the car. I would have run him over had I not heard him.

During one of our Santa outings, I spun out on I-71, sending the car careening several times before it hit the concrete barrier. A lady slowed down to yell out the window, "Watch out, you ass-holes!" as if I had planned to wreck the car on purpose. While there was some damage to the car, it was mostly fine—they were built like tanks back then. Dave, though, was bleeding like a stuck pig from a minor cut above his eye where he'd hit his head. We were close to his in-laws' house, so we stopped there and Dave's wife stitched him up. I jokingly offered to do it myself—after all,

Me with my friends George (dog costume) and Dave (Santa) plus my dog Gypsy. I always wore a beard so my kids wouldn't recognize me. My sister made my elf outfit; it doubled as a leprechaun costume in March.

my uncle was a doctor—but he stubbornly refused. "I think you've done enough to me for one night," he said.

We always started these evenings in great spirits, but the grueling schedule—sometimes getting home at 4 a.m.—wore us down. The late nights and lack of sleep took a toll, and our evenings ended with verbal exchanges like, "If you ring those damn bells in my ear one more time . . ." We all carried flashlights to help us find addresses, and one night, when frustration levels were at a peak, George yelled, "I've had enough of this shit!" and flung his flashlight out the window. Naturally, I tossed mine too, and so did Dave. And just like that, a tradition was born: the ceremonial flashlight toss. Each year on our final run, every single flashlight went out the window, saluting the end of the season.

PERKS

The Popular Kids Table

I don't really see myself as a celebrity. I'm just a regular guy who was fortunate to do something I loved. But I do recall the moment I realized I was more than a jeweler in Cleveland. Chuck, Dick Goddard, and I were walking down the hall at Channel 8 when Dick casually asked, "Did you guys know we made the Top Five Most Recognizable People in Cleveland list?"

It was no surprise to learn that Dick received such an honor. He had been on TV several nights a week for decades. But the more I thought about Chuck and me, the more unbelievable it seemed. I started reflecting on all the news anchors, not just on TV 8 but across all the Cleveland channels. They were all on multiple times a week during prime viewing hours. Chuck and I were then on the air only once a week, and late at night. And even when our show did air, we were on-air as hosts only for about twenty-five minutes, with the rest of the time dedicated to the movie and the skits. Then, I considered all the local sports players and their popularity. The more I thought about it, the more unbelievable it was. I never saw the rankings article, but I just assumed Goddard came in first. And that didn't stop me from teasing Chuck that I must have come in second, leaving him in third place. I argued that a guy who stands at eye level to your belly button must be more memorable!

In addition to moments of admiration, I've had several humbling moments as well. Sherry and I were at Geneva-on-the-Lake with some out-of-town friends, and Dr. G was laying it on thick, telling everyone what a big star I was in Cleveland. As we were walking to dinner, some girls on the other side of the street started waving and shouting excitedly in our direction. Being used to that kind of attention, I put on my "celebrity face" and prepared to proudly greet my eager fans in front of my guests—only to watch them run right past me and straight to Dr. G. Turns out, they worked at a restaurant he frequented and loved him for his outgoing personality and his very generous tipping. I laughed it off, but it was deflating.

I've always been grateful for my fans, and have enjoyed the personal interactions with them. While I'm used to being recognized around Cleveland, I'm still pleasantly surprised when people recognize me elsewhere—and I haven't been to many places where that doesn't happen. I've been stopped by fans all around the world.

While visiting Spain with my friend Dave, we had some free time one day, so we decided to take a boat across the Strait of Gibraltar to Africa. The way that boat smelled, I swear they were smuggling goats in the lower deck. The urinals in the bathroom were ridiculously high for me, so I had to awkwardly balance myself on a pipe to use them. While I was in this precarious position, a guy walked in and casually said, "Hey, Lil' John—Lakewood, Ohio."

While visiting Rome, I stood in front of a jewelry store called Rinaldi's Jewelry. Rinaldi is as popular a name in Italy as Smith is in the U.S. A guy walking by said, "Hey, Lil' John, how are you? What are you doing here?" I pointed to the sign and said, "Just checking up on my international branch."

Although I am often recognized locally, not everyone knows who Lil' John is, and I don't always receive special treatment. Once, I was attending an Indians game with my kids, and we had box seats right behind the dugout. My son was a huge Ken Griffey fan and wanted an autograph, so I jumped over the fence and grabbed a couple of balls lying on the ground. This was back when I could still get away with something like that. I saw Griffey and started walking toward him, but as soon as Griffey saw me, he began walking away. The faster he moved, the quicker I followed until I inadvertently chased him across the field and into the dugout. I'm sure to anyone watching this looked like a Benny Hill skit. As Griffey disappeared into the locker room, the manager stopped me at the dugout and said, "Griffey isn't signing anything today."

When I returned to my seat, an usher came over and said, "Herb Score wants to know why you were chasing Ken Griffey around the dugout like a lunatic." (Herb was the Indians' radio broadcaster.) I explained that I was trying to get an autograph for my kid. A couple of innings later, the usher returned and said, "Herb asked if you could come up to the press box." When I arrived, Herb asked again, "John, why were you chasing Griffey around the field?"—and then handed me a signed ball from Griffey.

Generous Gifts

I've never let my TV career go to my head, but I won't deny that I've enjoyed the perks that came with it. I've had opportunities to do things well beyond my financial means, and I'm grateful for every opportunity. I've never made a habit of asking for things, but I've always been happy to accept when something was offered. I often tell people I am a "country club whore"—if you invite me, I will definitely show up. So be sure you actually want me there, especially if there is food and drinks.

In my younger days, I had nosebleed seats for Browns games. But after getting to know someone high up in the Browns organization, I was invited to the private loge. Gone were the days of dressing for the cold weather; now I could drive into the stadium grounds, park in a private covered lot, and have an all-access pass to anywhere in the stadium. Instead of riding the private elevator straight to the loge with everyone else, though, I would take a longer route through the press box. Truth be told, I didn't mind if people noticed the credential around my neck—it was a badge of honor, and I liked being part of the inner circle.

Chuck and I were regularly inundated with T-shirts from various organizations we featured on the show. I gave most of mine away because they were too big. Chuck wrapped up many of his to give as Christmas presents. On-air, I once jokingly requested that if anyone wanted to send us clothes, please send pants or shoes; we had plenty of T-shirts. The following week, designer jeans showed up at the station. It turns out people did listen to us on the show!

Sometimes we received homemade food. I hesitated to eat it. I would bring my share home and set it aside, and when I spoke with Chuck a day or two later, I would ask, "Hey, how were those brownies?"

If he said, "Oh, they were delicious," and didn't mention becoming ill, I would eat mine. If he said "Oh, I gave it away," I didn't eat it.

Flight School

By the early 2000s, I had been on television for three decades and had become accustomed to—and remained grateful for—all the freebies that came along with my celebrity status: tickets to shows, drinks on the house, upgraded seats, and various other gestures of hospitality. However, this one was huge.

"You're pretty funny. How would you like to go to Michael Jordan's basketball camp?"

That was my new friend, Ed. We had just been introduced by a mutual friend over cigars and cocktails.

"Count me in," I said—not really giving the question much thought.

Ed then retrieved a camp brochure from his car and handed it to me. Even with my poor eyesight and the small print, I could make out the huge price tag.

"You've got the wrong guy; I would never pay that," I said.

"How would you like to go for free?"

"I should explain what free means to me," I said. "It means 'no charge.'"

"Your only cost would be your airfare to the camp and two meals on your own," Ed replied.

I thanked him, but I assumed the entire thing as a scam and let the matter drop.

About a month later, Ed called me at the jewelry store. "Hey John, you might want to check out airfare; it's low right now to Vegas."

"Can you tell me more about this? How exactly are you connected to the camp?"

"If you still have the brochure I gave you, look on page three," he said. Turns out, my new friend was the camp director. "John, just to show you I'm legit, why don't you come to my house for my March Madness party?"

"Thanks, but I don't want to fly anywhere now."

"Look at the address on page twenty-two of the brochure, that's my address." Ed was practically my neighbor, living just a few streets away.

At the party, I couldn't turn around without bumping into Mike Fratello, Bob Huggins or any number of other legendary basketball coaches. As I would eventually learn, Ed was a renowned and well-connected coach who ran camps nationwide, including Michael Jordan's Senior Flight School, an exclusive four-day basketball camp in Las Vegas for men age 35 and over.

I took Ed up on his offer and went.

I've enjoyed plenty of perks from being on TV locally, but attending Jordan's Flight School camp was a different level of

VIP. Guest were treated to the top-shelf of everything. A chauffeured limo greeted me at the airport. At the luxury hotel, I found goody bags full of basketball gear waiting for me. Anywhere I went, simply mentioning I was with Michael's camp whisked me to the front of the line, even into restaurants that were usually booked months in advance.

I wasn't there to play basketball, just to hang out. I was rubbing shoulders with legendary coaches like Mike Krzyzewski, John Thompson, Larry Brown, Bill Walton, and many others. Of course, the highlight of the camp was spending time with Michael Jordan, who would often gear up and join the games.

The first time I attended the camp, I mistakenly assumed I could just walk up to Michael Jordan for an autograph. I couldn't have been more wrong. Everything followed a strict schedule, especially interactions with MJ. For the photo sessions, an attendant would prep you five people deep, asking for your name, hometown, and a question for Michael. MJ would then greet you in line and make "personal" conversation using those notes as you both made your way to the photo op area.

On the elevator ride to our photo op, a guy on the elevator handed me a massive cigar, thinking it was hilarious to give the smallest guy the biggest smoke. I tucked it in my shirt pocket for later. During his own photo op, that same guy gave Michael a regular-sized cigar. When it was my turn for pictures, I said to Michael, "I know you like cigars," as I pulled the giant one from my pocket and handed it over.

He let out a laugh. "The biggest guy gave me the smallest cigar, and the littlest guy gave me the biggest one." It felt good to get a genuine laugh from Michael.

After the first couple of years of attending, I ditched the static photo shoots everyone else took. One year, I stood on a chair next to Michael; another year, I made him bend down so I could actually get my arm around him.

After five fantastic years of attending the camp, it finally came to an end in 2010. My wife says I almost cried when I found out—and she's right. A few years later, Sherry, Ed, and I went back to Vegas for vacation with some other friends. We had dinner at one of the upscale restaurants we frequented during the camp years. Back then, we always ordered the most expensive steak on the menu—the Wagyu. This time, as I looked at the menu—knowing the Rinaldi dime was covering the cost, not the camp—I wondered how I would tell the waiter I'd have a cheeseburger and fries in front of all my friends. Not only did I choose the Wagyu, but I also announced to everyone, "Order whatever you want, dinner is on me."

I am sure it was my imagination, but it seemed that suddenly everyone began ordering things they would not have otherwise asked for. Food and drinks kept coming and were spread across the table like a king's feast. I began to sweat. As dinner wound down, instead of thinking about what I might order for dessert, I was fixated on all the empty plates and glasses, mentally calculating how bad the damage would be. Just so there isn't any misunderstanding, it's not that I couldn't afford to or didn't want to treat my friends; I just hadn't mentally prepared for a bill that could double as a mortgage payment when I made the spontaneous gesture. As the dessert course concluded, I braced for the inevitable. But, like an angel from heaven, the manager came over to our table and announced, "Gentlemen and ladies, I hope you've enjoyed the evening—your meals are on the house." Ed still had a reputation in town, and the manager wanted to thank us for all the patronage over the years. What a relief!

License and Registration, Please

I need to preface this next story by stating that I have a very clean driving record. On our way to Florida one time, while driving through Virginia, I had an experience I wish had involved some celebrity recognition. At the very moment I was telling Sherry that her car was much faster than mine, blue lights began flashing in my rearview mirror. After I pulled to the side of the road, a large highway patrol officer approached my window and asked why I was in such a hurry. I explained we were on vacation and I was eager to get to Florida. After running my license, he returned with a ticket for speeding and reckless operation. Although I wasn't happy about the speeding, I was guilty and couldn't argue that. But I didn't understand the reckless operation. I told the officer I was simply keeping up with traffic and I wouldn't sign the ticket. He told me to sign it or I was going to jail. Reluctantly, I signed and threw my copy in the glove box. A few days later, I couldn't find the ticket. I called the highway patrol for help, but learned I needed to know which county had issued the ticket, which I didn't recall.

On our return trip home, I stopped at a Virginia visitor center to ask for a county map. When the clerk asked why, I explained my situation. Before I could finish my sentence, she said, "Wytheville," and quickly recited the courthouse phone number as if it were her own. She explained that Wytheville had a reputation as a speed trap. When I got home, I called the highway patrol again to clarify the situation. The person I spoke with told me I was lucky I wasn't in jail, and that a court appearance was mandatory—and she gave me my date. Confused, I said, "I don't understand. I was speeding; I didn't kill anyone."

I called a lawyer friend for advice, and he told me he would take care of it. However, an hour later, he called back and said I was in big trouble. He put me in touch with an attorney in Virginia who said he could assist with my case. The Virginia lawyer told me I needed to attend traffic school, provide three letters of recommendation attesting to my good character, and pay a fine. Hoping to make use of my local celebrity profile, I asked whether I should get letters from high-profile individuals, such as a chief of police or the Governor of Ohio. He said no; if you get letters from such powerful people, the judge will think you're trying to use your connections to avoid the consequences, and he will also think that's why you don't have any other tickets. He advised it's better to get letters from regular people.

I made my appointment at Parma Traffic School and arrived a little before 9 a.m. with forty other people. I quickly read the twelve-page booklet I was given. When the instructor arrived, I told her that I had finished reading the booklet and asked if I could take the test. She explained that I had to stay for the entire class, which would end at 5 p.m.

At 9 a.m. class began, and a camera scanned the room to ensure no one left early. The instructor started class by asking everyone to introduce themselves. The first woman explained that she had several DUIs and had fled to Florida. The next guy shared that he was busted with drugs, and when the police searched his house they found his meth lab. Another lady explained she was drunk and hit a telephone pole, which fell onto a school bus. Another older man explained he had lost his license and his ailing mother had to drive him to work.

Then it was my turn. "I'm John. I was speeding." The whole class went silent for what felt like forever. I think they were waiting for me to confess to running over a kid in a school parade or plowing my car through the front window of a restaurant. After a long pause, I finally added, "That's it."

Everyone in the room let out a mock "Ooh" as if I were a notorious criminal.

After the introductions, the instructor told us we could go next door to the convenience store for snacks or beverages. Knowing it would be a long, tedious day, I took advantage of it and kept getting up to buy snacks. Before long, my table overflowed with every imaginable snack. I was utterly frustrated being in this situation—at sixty years old, just for a speeding ticket.

After completing traffic school and getting my three letters of recommendation, I had to send a certified check for $1,000 to the attorney in Virginia, which my lawyer in Ohio handled on my behalf. My understanding was that this was the final piece to resolving the issue. Several months passed, and I didn't hear anything, so I called my attorney to confirm everything was handled. He told me he hadn't heard anything but would check into it and call me back.

Thirty minutes later, he called back, panicked. "John, you're in serious trouble. There's a warrant out for your arrest."

"WHAT? What are you talking about?" I replied.

"The lawyer in Virginia never received the check, so he never went to court. Since you missed your court date, a warrant was issued."

We eventually discovered that the attorney in Virginia had been using outdated letterhead with his old office address on it, and we had unknowingly sent the check to the wrong location. Fortunately, the check was found, and the attorney assured me he would go to court and explain the mix-up. In the meantime, I had Sherry drive everywhere. I was terrified that if I got pulled over, I'd end up in jail. Later that year, I saw a *60 Minutes* segment about Wytheville that confirmed what the clerk had told me about the town's notorious ticketing practices.

The other ticket I received was in Richfield, Ohio. I wasn't paying attention to my speed and was cited for the infraction. I couldn't tell if the officer was serious or a smart-ass when he asked, "Should I put 'TV star' or 'jewelry store owner' for occupation on the ticket?" I had to appear in the Cuyahoga Falls court. Since I knew everyone in that city, I decided to go early, hoping to run into someone I knew who might let me quickly pay my fine and be on my way. Unfortunately, it didn't turn out that way. I sat waiting for my court appearance like everyone else. As the place filled up, people began to recognize me, creating a commotion with laughter, conversation, and horseplay. Eventually, the bailiff called, "John Rinaldi, the judge wants to see you in his chambers."

"I can't have all this noise in the courthouse," the judge explained. "Let's get this sorted out right now. How do you plead?"

"Guilty," I said.

"Okay, go down the hall and pay your fine at the desk."

It turns out that's not the usual procedure for a guilty plea. After court proceedings, a guard is supposed to escort the person to the payment window. Since I went to the window without a guard, another commotion erupted. Just another day in the life!

To round out my collection of traffic stop adventures, here's one more. Late one evening, not far from my house, I got pulled over. I wasn't speeding and hadn't broken any traffic laws. The officer walked up to my already-rolled-down window, took one look at me, and immediately started apologizing.

"Oh—sorry, sir. Please disregard the traffic stop," he said as he began to walk away.

I wasn't upset—just curious—so I asked politely, "Why did you stop me?"

Clearly embarrassed, he replied, "I . . . uh . . . didn't see anyone driving. I thought a kid had stolen a car and was going for a joyride."

WITH FRIENDS LIKE THESE . . .

Being on television for five decades never felt like work—it was more like one continuous comedy sketch. That was pretty much true for my life off-camera, too. I have always been surrounded by friends connected by laughter and unapologetic smart-assery—and a relentless dedication to pranks.

George

George was one of my oldest friends, and we constantly fought over who'd pick up the check at lunch or dinner. One time I paid and forced his twenty-dollar bill back into his hand. A couple of days later, he told me he'd paid me back—by hiding the twenty-dollar bill somewhere in my apartment. This led to a lifelong game of hide-and-seek with the same bill. It got so competitive that we wrote down the serial number to ensure that neither of us cheated by slipping a different bill into the game. We also made a rule that George couldn't hide it more than three feet above my head.

George and I owned several used boats together, and we had a hell of a time with them. We rammed the first one into another boat because we'd installed the steering mechanism backward. Someone shot a hole in our second boat, and it sank to the bottom of Lake Erie. We mainly used our boats for fishing, but occasionally we'd stay overnight at Marblehead or Kelleys Island. Since those spots were usually filled with families or vacationing couples, we'd

I've always been surrounded with friends sharing an offbeat sense of humor. Here I am with good friends George and Dave: Hear no evil, see no evil (one-eyed version, anyway), and see no evil—again. We just couldn't get it right.

play the jokesters, spinning ridiculous stories about how we were hiding out from our wives, who liked to beat us up. Of course, the jig was up the moment our lovely wives actually joined us.

When George was in the hospital recovering from throat surgery, I was able to visit him after hours, thanks to my local celebrity status. When I asked if he needed anything, he didn't hesitate: "A vodka martini would be great." Being a good friend and a bad influence, I smuggled the vodka in. George asked the nurse to bring us two cups of ice, which she did, along with a pitcher of water that she assumed we also needed. We slipped out by the elevators to enjoy our drinks. All went well until George took a sip. He immediately started choking, turning all shades of red and purple. Panicked, we dumped the evidence down a gap in the floor just seconds before the nurse arrived. George was promptly discharged the next day.

Hospitals are prime territory for pranks. When my friend Don was immobilized in his hospital bed after surgery, I knew he was a sitting duck. Don enjoyed his evening cocktails, so on our first visit, a couple of our mutual friends and I left several airline-sized miniature bottles of booze at the foot of his bed—just out of his reach. We upped the ante the next time, leaving several raunchy adult magazines at his feet. This time, we hit the nurse's call button and left in a hurry, leaving him with the fallout of explaining.

I've kept up with the times and upgraded my pranks using new tech. If you're one of my close friends, don't be shocked if you're jolted awake at 3 a.m. by a command given to your Alexa to play The Star-Spangled Banner loudly. Of course, my friends instantly know who did it, so I'll get a call at 3:05 a.m.

Dr. G

When I first met Dr. G. he developed a habit of bending down to talk to me. After a while, I finally snapped, "I'm short, not deaf!" He laughed, which is why we became fast friends. I've always gravitated toward people who share my style of humor. At the finest restaurants, Dr. G curiously asks the server if the menu prices are for two or four people, and whether they're negotiable. With a generous heart, he rarely lets his guests touch the dinner check, but once it arrives, he performs a theatrical audit. "Okay, who had the extra onions for a dollar ninety-eight?"

Dr. G was a solid basketball player, so when he asked to join the All-Star team, it was an easy decision. Shortly after he joined, he played a terrific prank on the entire team. During player announcements before the game, when Dr. G was announced the applause from the crowd was deafening—it rivaled the cheers Chuck and I got! I was baffled because Dr. G wasn't a celebrity or a public figure. So after this happened at several games, I asked the friend he always brought along with him. She said, "He buys dozens of T-shirts and asks me to hand them out to the crowd and tell them to cheer like crazy when Dr. G is introduced." (He also made sure kids, especially those with disabilities, got a shirt.)

My friends and I share a lot of laughter but we do disagree now and then, although it rarely gets heated. One time, though, during dinner at a restaurant with Dr. G, I got so angry with him that I grabbed my coat and barked at Sherry, "We're leaving. Let's go!" I was so enraged as I stormed out that I didn't even notice my wife hadn't moved from her seat.

Three minutes later I walked back in and silently sat back down. Sherry still hadn't moved.

"Why are you back?" Dr. G casually asked—clearly enjoying my return walk of shame.

"You drove!"

The Secret Rinaldi Society

A chosen family of friends makes the good times better and the bad times shorter—and I had exactly that kind of group.

It started with five friends dropping by the jewelry store every Saturday to read the paper and bullshit about the week's events. I was there to work, but Saturdays were slow, so we eventually started ordering in lunch. Eventually, it turned into a club, and in 1987 the Secret Rinaldi Society was formalized. We had member jackets custom-made and we chartered rules. Fines were levied for various infractions, such as missing a meeting without calling.

The group consisted of Dr. G, Nathan, Jerry "the C", Rich, me, and Dr. Robert White, the world-renowned neurosurgeon from MetroHealth Medical Center. Dr. White was a major figure in the field of medicine, a public speaker, and a Nobel Prize nominee. I'll

Friends make the good times better and the bad times shorter. The Secret Rinaldi Society had rules, stylish jackets, and one member who was a Nobel Prize nominee. (Not me, in case you were wondering.) *(Linda Meyer)*

never forget the time he called me from Russia to ask if I could retrieve a manuscript he had left at home and take it to the airport. A jet was waiting to fly it to Russia.

I met Dr. White while working at Cowell & Hubbard, where he was a regular customer. When he visited, usually with one or more of his ten kids, he would announce in his booming voice, "Children, it's not a crime to steal; it's only a crime if you get caught." With that sense of humor, we hit it off immediately. It was Dr. White's idea to formalize our Saturday meeting into a club, and he suggested the name since we met at my store. Despite his busy schedule, he was a stickler for the rules. Even though it was a ten-dollar phone call from Russia to let me know he couldn't make a meeting, he followed the rule to avoid the two-dollar fine for being absent.

Dr. White made several memorable appearances on *The Big*

Chuck & Lil John Show, often playing a doctor. He was one of the most fascinating individuals I've ever known, and I was honored to give his eulogy in 2010.

The Rinaldi Society has met every week since 1987, with occasional breaks and a few changes in membership over the years. In case you were wondering what we discuss each week, per society rules, I can't tell you. As they say in spy novels, the less you know, the better off you are—and if I told you, then I'd have to kill you.

THINGS CHANGE, SO I KEEP MOVING

All Things Come to an End

The first two decades of the twenty-first century brought many changes to my life. In downtown Cleveland, a Euclid Avenue improvement project was underway, lasting several years. The construction in front of my jewelry store made it difficult for shoppers to get in my door, and the constant noise didn't create the calm, relaxed environment I wanted. Also, the employee base downtown was shrinking, contributing to declining sales. It was time for a change. After twenty-four years on East 9th Street, I relocated to Solon in 2004.

The changes continued. Technology and the internet were racing ahead, and for retail owners like me that really was a double-edged sword. Having a cell phone and GPS made my personal life easier and more efficient, but the internet completely changed how people shopped. Jewelry customers were evolving, and so were their expectations. More and more people came in to the store to pick my brain only to leave and order their jewelry online. They didn't want the personal, romantic experience I had always loved giving.

I never regretted becoming a jeweler—I enjoyed sharing what I knew and helping people find the perfect gift. And let's be honest, no one has ever gotten a hernia lifting a diamond. But eventually I could see the time had come to call it quits. After fifty years in the jewelry business, Sherry and I officially closed the store on February 14, 2017. I still help close friends and family with their jewelry needs, but store ownership is behind me, and I've never looked back.

I've learned to embrace change and keep moving. Staying busy has been my secret to navigating life's twists and turns with a positive attitude, and I wouldn't have it any other way.

A Great Cast Is Worth Repeating

In the mid-1990s, Fox Broadcasting acquired WJW, and soon after, major decisions were made solely by Fox executives who were not from Cleveland and had no knowledge of local legends Big Chuck and Lil' John. Various changes in station management affected the show, and in particular our time slot was frequently moved. Despite receiving minimal notice of the change in airtime—other than announcements Chuck and I ourselves made during the show—our loyal viewers always found us and tuned in.

The show continued to have consistently strong ratings, but by the mid-2000s, it was clear that the Fox executives wanted uniform programming across all its affiliate networks, leaving no room for a local show like ours.

Besides the station ownership change, other aspects of the show had changed as well. The grassroots feel was gone. It became nearly impossible to connect with local athletes to be part of our show because their own celebrity status had increased so much. Other access Chuck once had was no longer available. In the early days, Chuck had been able to secure almost anything he needed with just a phone call. He could arrange for a Greyhound bus, entry to restricted areas of buildings, and a road to be temporarily closed as easily as ordering a pizza. Not any more. By the late 1990s, even

Members of the dream team behind *The Big Chuck and Lil' John Show*: Jim Szymanski, Bill Ward, Tom Bush, Art Lofredo, Big Chuck, and me.

the horror and sci-fi genre movies we had featured for years were disappearing. Fox had licensing deals for bigger-budget, higher-production-quality movies with major stars. Instead of *Little Shop of Horrors* or *Silent Running* (one of Chuck's favorites), the station was airing *Mr. Mom*, *A Fish Called Wanda*, and *Rocky*. Chuck and I had no control over that. I personally didn't care which movie aired because I didn't see them during taping, and with my busy schedule, I seldom watched the show when it aired. But I knew fans loved those genre movies and were disappointed when they were no longer shown.

The final regular episode of *The Big Chuck & Lil' John Show* aired on June 16th, 2007. The hosting segments were recorded with the cast and friends in Chuck's basement rec room. The following week, an hour-long retrospective titled "End of an Era" aired, allowing Chuck and me to offer an intimate goodbye to our fans, highlighting memorable moments. This brought an incredible chapter of my life to a close—or so I thought.

As disappointed as I was about the show going off the air, it didn't change my life much. Chuck and I continued making personal appearances just as often as before, and I was still managing the jewelry store full-time. The transition was probably more challenging for Chuck. Without the responsibility of producing the show—a massive undertaking each week—he had more free time. What likely helped ease his transition was that he was busy writing a book of memoirs and preparing for its upcoming release.

We were fortunate to have worked with so many talented individuals.

Bob Wells was the most experienced regular on the show and a real on-air TV professional. I would have been a star if I had even half of his talent. I liked Hoolie a lot, but I loved him when he left, because I got his job.

Art Lofredo was another standout. Though quiet off-camera, he had a remarkable ability to transform into any character in front of the camera and was a brilliant technician behind the scenes. After Hoolie, Chuck, and me, Art was the most prominent member of the cast.

Bill Ward was a fantastic producer and director with a storied career that included work in Hollywood and radio. He appeared in several fan favorite skits and was often heard on our show doing announcing and voice-over work.

Mary Allen, who often played Chuck's wife in skits, was incredibly talented and outgoing. We had a great time whenever we were together. I fondly remember a night in Vegas when I returned to the hotel late one evening at the same time Mary Allen was walking in, appearing as though she and her friend had the time of their lives.

Tom Bush joined the cast in the 1970s and was exceptional at impersonations, performing many memorable ones on the show, including John Wayne, George Bush, and Jimmy Carter.

Jim Szymanski, a local radio personality, joined the show shortly before I started co-hosting. With his great speaking voice, he did an excellent job as our in-house Ed McMahon, getting the live audience seated, warmed up, and ready to laugh. Jim also made appearances in several fan-favorite skits.

Julie Ann Cashel was an absolute sweetheart. A talented local actress, dancer, and model, she joined the cast and often played characters that required beauty and a shapely figure; she became known on the show and to fans as "Julie Ann Goodbody." Probably her best-known role was "Blunder Woman" in our parody of the popular TV show *Wonder Woman*. I used to tease her because I never saw her eat, even at events where free food was served. One day, I asked her why she didn't eat, and she explained that she didn't want anything stuck in her teeth. (Considering her modeling background, I assumed she always tried to look her best.) I told her I'd let her know if that happened, and assured her the food was delicious. She flashed one of her brilliant smiles at me, and we ate lunch together that day.

Dick Goddard was a meteorologist for six decades and one of the biggest names in Cleveland. He was also a natural in front of the camera and loved being in skits. He was also a talented singer, having appeared in several musicals during his high school years. I recall one occasion, just before the news was about to air, when the program director kept calling for Dick to be on set. Chuck and I were in the hall, watching as Dick walked by awkwardly, seemingly distracted by something. I told him he was needed on set, and he replied, "I know, just a minute." We watched as he made his way to the back door, opened it, and let a spider out. That was Dick—always considerate, even to the smallest creatures.

Herb Thomas started at TV 8 cleaning up, then moved to the printing room and eventually became one of our best camera-

Herb "Soul Man" Thomas was a giant in stature, personality, and kindness. Herb worked at Channel 8 in various roles before eventually becoming a camera operator. He appeared in many skits on our show.

men. His skits as Soulman are still among the most loved by fans. Outside the show, Herb played congas in a popular local band, The Prayer Warriors. It was a tragedy that he passed away so young.

During the run of the show, Fox8 hosted two memorable parties. A 25th anniversary party in 1988 was held at Shorty's Diner, a 1950s-themed restaurant in the Flats. Shirts were made, and assorted gifts were given, like white socks with the outlines of Chuck and me. Our farewell party in 2007 was held at the downtown Hilton, and I must give credit: it was a top-notch affair with approximately 250 attendees, including family, friends, and Fox8 employees. We did a question-and-answer session, and after every couple of questions, I announced, "Chuck might be retiring, but I'm not." It was a great party, but honestly, I wish they'd spent the money on extending our TV show for another year or two instead.

Back But Not the Same

I was sure the station would eventually ask Chuck and me to bring the show back on-air. At the risk of sounding arrogant, we were still among the most recognizable faces in Cleveland. We were living, breathing advertisements for the station, and our presence generated significant goodwill, not to mention the effortless sellouts of commercial airtime during our show. It took a few years, but in 2011 Fox8 finally asked us to host a new show—thirty minutes, skits only.

I was happy to be back on the air, but the new show was different and not much fun to shoot. With the previous show, we had a crew of about five people and shot with several cameras. Having the crew made shooting more enjoyable. We had people to interact with, and we genuinely enjoyed our relationships with them. For the new show, it was just Chuck and me in front of a single stationary camera and a crew of one. The camera was locked in a fixed position, and the lone crew person managed the teleprompter. We began filming three shows at a time, but eventually cranked out ten at a time, which I didn't mind because that way I only had to show up at the studio once every ten weeks.

The most significant difference between the two shows was the absence of a live studio audience. I missed that. Comedy thrives on the energy and feedback of the audience; their laughter and reactions help gauge what works and doesn't. Without that chorus of laughter, the show felt sterile and lifeless—it was much like what I imagine it would be like performing to the resident audience of a morgue.

For decades, Chuck had had complete control over which skits aired, but that, too, gradually ended, at least in part because the studio deemed many of our old skits socially or politically incorrect and wouldn't allow them to be shown. By the time we transitioned to the new 30-minute show, the list of available skits had become limited, and skits were frequently repeated. Comedy reflects the times, and it evolves whether we want it to or not. What was harmless fun decades ago can land very differently today, and I understand that. Looking back, some of the older skits might seem outdated or even offensive through a modern lens. But in their moment, they were meant to make people laugh, nothing more. There was never any malice behind them, just an attempt to entertain with the kind of humor that fit the era.

Although I'm the last person who would want to offend anyone or be insensitive, I can't help but wish we hadn't collectively lost the ability to laugh at ourselves. At just over four feet tall, I've learned something about maintaining a sense of humor regarding sensitive subjects. Life is too short—and so am I—not to find some humor in our quirks, differences, and imperfections.

Covid Killed It

In 2020, COVID-19 restrictions forced the studio to shut down, and we ceased producing new shows. For a while, reruns aired, but eventually the show's format shifted to just showing skits with no hosting segments.

COVID-19 also temporarily ended personal appearances, including one lucrative promotional gig I especially enjoyed. Around 2017, a representative from a local alcohol distributor contacted me about helping promote alcoholic beverages at local restaurants and bars. My job was to provide entertainment and help with giveaways. Two young, attractive ladies accompanied me and handed out samples of that evening's product. The first event took place at a venue in Parma. I suggested to the girls, "How about you put a T-shirt on over what you're wearing? Then, I'll tell the crowd that whoever answers the next trivia question correctly gets to remove your shirt."

"I'm not doing that!" one of the girls quickly said.

Surprised, I asked, "Why not?"

"She's got a better body than mine and will get picked every time," she said.

The second girl said, "I won't do it either."

"Why not?" I asked, surprised. "You've got your clothes on underneath the T-shirt."

"If I keep taking my shirt off, I'll mess up my hair," she said.

"Ladies, we're starting on the wrong foot," I calmly explained. "My routine is about humor; you know who I am, right? I need to do something funny."

Reluctantly, they agreed to go along with the suggestions—and the crowd went wild. After that, we got along very well and the girls were always open to my ideas. Each week, I worked with different girls, and as word spread, the promoter told me that all the girls were now eager to work with me because they were having so much fun.

Some of the beverages I promoted weren't exactly highbrow, and occasionally, when I offered someone a free beer, they'd turn it down.

"I'm not drinking that; it tastes like piss."

Being someone who's never at a loss for words, I'd ask, "How many beers have you had already?"

"Maybe four or five," they'd reply.

"If you've had that many, you're not going to taste the difference anyway. Plus, it's free!"

Chuck permanently retired from public appearances during the COVID-19 pandemic, and I feared that his retirement might also signal the end of mine. After all, we were a team, and that's how the public knew us. However, to my surprise, when personal appearances began to pick up again after COVID-19 restrictions were lifted, and I informed event sponsors that Chuck was unavailable, they still welcomed me to their events solo. I was both flattered and grateful. Events gradually resumed, but they never fully returned to pre-pandemic levels.

Did I Overstay My Welcome?

For about fifteen years, Sherry and I vacationed in Florida for a few weeks each year. We stayed with friends, but that arrangement became cumbersome, so we needed something else. I proposed a deal to my friends: I would be happy to visit their homes, but only at times when they wouldn't be there. I'd go on to explain that I'd need the last four digits of their Social Security number, as well as their passwords and codes for things like their cable TV and security systems. Finally, if they had a car on the property, I would need the keys because it would be inconvenient for me to rent one. After plenty of laughing, they agreed.

Before you think I'm a selfish jerk and this was some one-sided arrangement, let me clarify. I often traveled with a very handy buddy, and in exchange for our accommodations we'd do odd jobs and maintenance around the house at the start of each visit. We handled everything from changing light bulbs to repairing storm-damaged fences and addressing anything else that needed attention. Plus, people appreciated having someone check on their homes so they did not sit empty for long periods. Our reputation for getting things done spread, and soon people started asking us to stay at their place. Keep in mind that some of these properties were million-dollar places, and the list of repairs could be extensive.

I visited one friend's place so often that I put my name on the outside door, which led everyone to believe I lived there. I was invited to country clubs and was frequently greeted by other members— "Hi, Mr. Rinaldi! How are you?" That usually sparked a remark from my annoyed companion, who was the official member, "Nobody said hi to *me*!"

Eventually, our stays became longer, and staying in the same house for the entire visit was no longer feasible, and moving from one home to another—one week here, another week there—wasn't ideal, so Sherry and I decided to buy a property of our own. That decision was unpopular among our friends who didn't want to lose the caretaking services.

Full-Time Flip Flops

We visited a house that was being sold due to the owner's health issues. We liked the house, and I inquired about the neighborhood and parking for guests. The seller's agent, who lived in the development, told us the neighborhood didn't like disruptive activity or parties and implied that people like my wife and I weren't welcome. I'm not easily offended, but this remark rubbed me the wrong way. Naturally, I bid on the house, and I told my wife that if the offer was accepted, I would decorate the entire home inside and out with Christmas lights, and we'd host parties every weekend. Not surprisingly, our offer was declined. We eventually found the perfect house and got the keys in January 2010. Sherry and I had been looking forward to enjoying the mild weather in our new winter home, but it turned out to be one of the coldest winters the state had experienced, with frozen geckos falling from the trees.

Out-of-Town Wife, Out-of-Control Life

Having retired from the jewelry business and with no more obligations to the TV show, I now had all the time in the world to do whatever I wanted, but I'm not one to sit idle. And even though I am now 80, I'm still not ready to act my age. Sure, I engage in a few classic older-person activities—Sherry and I enjoy working on puzzles, and I like doing the jumble. And maybe someday, when I'm old, I'll kick back lounging in pajamas, binge-watching TV. But for now, I'm determined to make the most of every day. I keep a busy calendar, jotting down things I want to do, and it's common to find me out with friends for lunch or dinner.

Every few years, I like to mix things up just for fun. When I turned sixty-five, my good friend Bill approached me with a question.

"How long have we been friends, John?"

"About thirty years," I replied.

"Well, that's long enough, then. I have to tell you something I don't like about you."

"Really? What's that?"

"Your teeth."

"Well, you're an orthodontist," I shot back. "Put some braces on them!"

Bill had already put them on my children's teeth and my grandchildren's teeth. And so, at sixty-five, I became the oldest—and the last—person in my family to get braces.

I've been a cigar fan most of my life, but at 70, I decided to give them up. At 75, I stopped dyeing my hair, and it was gray from then on. Life's too short not to shake things up once in a while!

As my eyesight changed with age, a couple of incidents convinced me that I should no longer drive at night. Sherry and I were leaving a friend's wedding at the country club, and I started

Sherry and I enjoy the good life in Florida—part of the year, at least. We decided that one hurricane was enough, though, so we skip those.

driving down what I thought was the exit road, but it seemed narrower than when we arrived. After passing by what appeared to be a ball washer, I realized I was several hundred feet down the golf course's cart path. I backed out, to avoid turning the car around and potentially leaving tire marks on the pristine grass. Not the impression I wanted to leave at a fancy country club.

Retirement has allowed us to spend several months each year at our Florida home. We prefer to fly, but with our dog, Rudy, joining the family, we drive so he can come with us. Sherry and I like listening to audiobooks, but finding books we both like can be challenging.

Occasionally, Sherry heads to Florida ahead of me, and when that happens, something usually goes wrong while I'm home alone. After a late evening out with my brother, I pulled into the garage only to find the door to the house locked. It was too late to call anyone without risking waking them up, so I resigned myself to a night in the car. Bundled in a garage blanket, I reassured myself that several people had a spare key and I'd sort it out in the morning.

My first stop in the morning was the neighbor's house. He retrieved the envelope labeled "John's spare key," but it was empty. He remembered my son had borrowed it a while back and never returned it. I called my son John, who was in Florida with my wife. "Sure, Dad, I've got a spare key, but it's on my keychain, which is in my pocket."

On to my other son, Dino, who worked just down the street. I drove to his workplace only to learn he'd taken the weekend off to go rafting in West Virginia. Out of options, I called Sherry, who suggested calling Frances, who had been our housekeeper for twenty years and had a key. I know this might sound odd, but I didn't know Frances's last name or phone number. Sherry called her, and thankfully, she saved the day.

I wish I could say this was a one-time event, but I got locked out again. That time, Solon police helped by opening the door faster than I could with a key.

On another occasion when Sherry was out of town, I woke up in the morning feeling like I'd been shot. I had a little red dot on my skin and thought it was a spider bite. But the pain worsened, so I made a trip to the doctor and found out I had shingles. That was some of the worst pain I've ever experienced. If you ever want to know what it feels like to be on fire and stabbed simultaneously, shingles will do just that!

The worst home-alone fiasco involved our dog, Rudy. I like Rudy, but there is no mistaking the fact that Rudy is Sherry's dog. Sometimes he gets more affection from Sherry than I do. I was taking Sherry to the airport about 4 p.m., and the last thing she said was, "Take good care of Rudy." The round-trip took about ninety minutes. As soon as I got home and stepped inside, something blue on the floor caught my eye. It was Rudy's pill bottle—he takes allergy meds. This was the same bottle that had sat on the counter for three years that the dog had never touched. But today, Rudy decided to knock it down—and help himself to every last pill. It was Sunday evening, and no vet offices were open. Panic struck, and my brain immediately went into overdrive, conjuring a cascade of increasingly ridiculous yet, at the time, entirely plausible thoughts. If Rudy doesn't make it, how fast could I get another dog that looks just like him? Would Sherry even notice? If worse came to worst, should I say he ran away? How much trouble would I be in if she found out?

Then I came up with a winning idea. When a person overdoses, you're supposed to walk them around or put them in a cold shower. I skipped the shower, but Rudy and I went for a walk.

When Sherry landed in Florida, she called right away, and the first thing she asked was "How's Rudy?" I said, as casually as possible, "Oh, we just got back from a nice long walk." Meanwhile, in the background, Rudy was hacking like he'd swallowed a chicken bone, but, thank God, Sherry didn't hear that. I didn't sleep much that night, waking every few minutes to check on Rudy. I was at the vet's office promptly at 8 a.m. The vet asked how many pills were left in the bottle. None, I said. The vet determined he had eaten about thirty pills based on when the prescription was issued and how many he should have taken each day. After the vet called the pill manufacturer, I was told he'd be fine—but to expect vomiting and diarrhea. I've never been so relieved. Now that I knew everything would be okay, I called Sherry to explain.

"I have something to tell you about Rudy," I said.

Her immediate response: "He's dead! Is Rudy dead?"

"No, he's fine," I reassured her, but she wasn't convinced.

"John, if he's really okay, take a picture of him with today's date on a piece of paper and send it to me."

I did as she asked and held the paper in front of Rudy like I was a terrorist delivering a ransom demand. Needless to say, Rudy got more sympathy from Sherry than I did. In my mind, I kept him alive . . . and I'm pretty sure that counts as taking good care of him.

Let's Take the Party South 1,200 Miles

I enjoy an active social life in Florida just as much as I do in Cleveland. The ironic thing is that it's with many of the same friends from Cleveland, including my brother. They all migrate south for the winter, and many live just a short drive from us in Florida. Having longtime friends nearby, however, doesn't stop me from expanding my social circle. A few years ago, I discovered a place called Showfolks near our house in Sarasota. I learned it was a social organization and bar exclusive to people who worked at or were associated with the circus. Once a year, they hold an open house where visitors can browse photos of past and present circus performances and see live acts. During one of these open houses, I inquired about membership. The lady behind the bar told me members must have been in the circus and needed two sponsoring members. I explained I had been a ringmaster several times and attended clown school. Chuckles the clown happened to be there that day, and I knew him from his visits to Cleveland; he said he would sponsor me. The lady behind the bar suggested that since it was almost the end of the year, I should return after January 1st to avoid paying the annual dues for just the few weeks left. When I returned, a different woman informed me that I couldn't join. Despite explaining my qualifications again, I was still turned away. A guy at one of the tables intervened and said, "He's okay; let him in." He was the president of the organization. I love hearing the stories the performers share. Still, they know I'm not a lifelong circus performer and I haven't quite cracked into the inner circle, but I hope one day they'll accept me as one of their own.

We are usually in Florida by October, and in 2024 we were

Another day in paradise. By the way, this is not one of the boats my friend George and I owned—which is why it is still floating.

there when Hurricane Milton hit. We chose to stay and ride out the storm. Before you raise an eyebrow, our house isn't in a flood zone, is at the highest elevation in Sarasota, and wasn't in an evacuation area. After I secured the storm shutters to the house (a task I usually hire out but could find nobody to do on short notice), there were other priorities. I checked the flashlight batteries, filled the bathtub (water for flushing the toilet), and ensured we had a few days' worth of groceries. I also made sure to stock up on snacks, stopping at the donut shop and hitting the liquor store for good measure. Because, you know, when you're trying to survive a hurricane, nothing says "I'm prepared" like donuts and a martini! Although we lost electricity for about eight hours, the hurricane never got as bad as predicted. Still, Sherry and I decided we won't be weathering another storm. Once was enough.

THAT'S A WRAP

Happiness, It's an Attitude

I warned you at the beginning of this book that you wouldn't find any profound revelations in these pages. But if you were still hoping for something more than stories of foolishness and absurdity from my life, stay with me; there is hope in this final chapter.

While writing this book, I was asked what life lessons I've learned. I replied that there weren't any life lessons; I just wanted to enjoy life and have a good time. But . . . maybe that *is* the life lesson—at least the lesson that was right for me.

Maintaining a sense of humor and not taking myself too seriously have always been important to me, especially at four feet three inches. I've learned to roll with whatever life throws at me and always find a reason to laugh. I have a knack for finding humor in everything. My wife sometimes reminds me that not everything is funny or a joke. But I reply, "Yes, yes, it is!" No matter where I am, funny thoughts are constantly swirling in my head, even in situations where most people struggle to find humor. Let's say I'm not great at funerals or hospitals, where I've learned it's best to keep my mouth shut and not let the voice in my head speak!

I've met people who knew me from TV but didn't understand my sense of humor and asked if I don't feel embarrassed about acting silly my whole life. My answer is always the same: "Not at all! That silliness put my kids through college and gave my wife and me a wonderful life!"

I never wake up expecting a bad day, and I never go places

Happiness is an attitude. I've always believed that—which is why you'll always find me wearing the same big smile.

expecting a bad time. I wake up expecting it to be the best day yet, and when I leave the house, I am determined to have a great time. My friend, Dr. G, who worked in the same building on East 9th Street where my jewelry store was, would stop by several times a day to say hello. One day, he asked if I knew why he stopped by so often. He told me it's because I'm always happy, and it's like a little ray of sunshine every time he comes by.

I'd be lying if I said I haven't had my share of heartbreaks and disappointment, but despite any unfair or randomly cruel punches life has thrown at me, I don't stay sad for long. I've held onto the belief that no matter what happens, the good outweighs the bad, and that's certainly been true in my life.

Being happy and having a good attitude are not just my natural state; they are conscious choices I make every day.

Luck Might Knock, But Choice Answers

I know most things in my life resulted from choices I made when opportunities presented themselves. Sure, luck and timing can matter—it was luck that Dick Blake walked into the jewelry store where I was working and I happened to be the one to assist him. But my long TV career began when I responded, "Yes" when he offered to introduce me to Big Chuck. An open mind and being ready for the moment mattered even more than luck, and those things played a significant role in the successes I've had my entire life.

Sure, taking chances and trying something new comes with a risk of failing, and, trust me, plenty of times things did not go the way I planned. But if you're not willing to step out of your comfort zone, nothing new or exciting ever happens. I've never set out to fail at anything, but when I did fail, I looked at it as a chance to learn—not a reason to give up. Besides, most of the time, the worst-case scenarios we imagine are way worse than what actually happens, even when things don't go as planned. If I had let fear of failure stop me, I would've missed out on a lot.

Through the Lens of Time

I've also thought a lot about family and friends while writing this book. It would be hard not to, right? My parents have been gone for many years, but I think about how blessed my life was with a close-knit extended family, and siblings who genuinely care about one another. My two siblings and I are five years apart, with me in the middle. Growing up, we were always at different life stages, creating a natural distance between us. I think that's one of the reasons we didn't fight much. But as we grew older, the age gap

My parents, Michael and Anna Rinaldi. Both came from large Italian families and were among the first in their families to be born in the U.S. family was always important to them, as it still is to me.

between us became meaningless and we grew closer. My brother and I really got to know each other as adults when I started college at OSU and he was still finishing his dentistry degree, and we had time to hang out. He is one of my lifelong best friends.

Stories I shared about my kids seem like they happened yesterday, but they were a lifetime ago. One minute you're wrestling with diapers and the next you're waving goodbye as they head off to start their independent lives. Time has flown by, and along the way, our family has grown to include some genuinely wonderful grandchildren: Onid (that's Dino spelled backward), Bruno, Abbey, Evan, and Elena, along with a terrific daughter-in-law, Ania. Both John and Dino stayed in the area and have grown into the people they always dreamed of being: When they were very young, both kids said they wanted to be like Mommy when they grew up—tall!

My mother-in-law, June, comes to mind any time I think of Christmas. She bought gifts for everyone, and everyone got more

Sherry and I raised two fantastic boys, John (top) and Dino (bottom left). To be honest, Sherry did way more than her share of the raising while I was running the store, handling my responsibilities for the show, and making personal appearances.

than one. The house was packed relatives, significant others, and kids. I wondered if some of the kids had wandered in off the street just to get a gift. It took hours to hand out the hundreds of presents because my father-in-law, Nick, insisted in doing so one by one. Back then, it sometimes seemed like a marathon, but I'd love nothing more than the chance to do it one more time with loved ones who are no longer here.

I particularly remember one gift from my mother-in-law. When Sherry and I were dating, June gave me a nutcracker. I thanked her and told her how much I liked it—which I genuinely did. After she told everyone in the family how much I enjoyed it, the floodgates opened. Every gift-giver jumped on board, and after a few Christmases, I had more nutcrackers than I could count. Fast-forward to today, and my collection has grown to enormous proportions. I display them all every year and in an orderly fashion. I like to picture them as my personal nutcracker army, standing guard for the holidays. What began decades ago as a single sweet gift has evolved into a full-fledged lifelong commitment. That taught me to be careful about what I tell people I like. I can't afford to tell anyone I like snow globes, which, for the record, I don't, but I do like hundred-dollar bills.

Now that both sets of our parents are gone, Sherry and I have settled into new traditions.

Perhaps the most anticipated holiday event is when our family gathers a couple of weeks before the holiday for the Great Ravioli Making, where we follow Mom's recipe carefully. Picture Santa's workshop, but we're cranking out 1,500 ravioli instead of toys. My brother and his wife do the bulk of the work. They make the meat, the dough and the sauce, and the remainder of the group is charged with assembly. We use a bit of modern mechanical help—no one's rolling them by hand anymore. These raviolis are the star of our Christmas Day meal and it's a serious business. You can eat as many as you'd like, but leaving any on your plate uneaten is a crime. It makes me happy that my family and I continue this childhood tradition. While we cook and enjoy each other's company, we dine on an assortment of appetizers and bottles of Rinaldi Barolo wine, no relation. I enjoy drinking this wine with family and giving it as a gift at holiday gatherings because it doesn't need a name tag—everyone knows who it's from.

Giving Back

Beyond the laughs I got at the time, it's incredibly meaningful to know that my work touched people's lives in ways I never

Cleveland has been incredibly good to me, and I've always been eager to give back whenever possible. Here I am at one of many fundraising events Chuck and I hosted for the Muscular Dystrophy Association.

expected. Over the years, fans have shared stories that moved me to tears. I've been told, "You changed my life" by people who shared memories of tough or abusive childhoods, describing how, for those two hours the show was on, they felt safe and that things were okay for a little while.

I've realized that when fans share memories with me, they're not just speaking to me—they're talking to themselves, reminiscing about their cherished Friday nights spent with family and friends. I can see the emotion on their face and hear it in their voice when they say, "My dad passed years ago, but we always watched together on Friday nights; those nights were some of the best memories of my life." It took me a long time to realize how much the show meant to so many people. The stories, kind words, and warm handshakes from fans have made me understand I did something meaningful and I'm grateful to have been part of so many lives.

I've always been willing to give back and support a town and people who have been so good to me. Through our joint efforts and my own work, Chuck and I raised millions of dollars for various charities—something I am deeply proud of.

I've also spent time visiting children with terminal illnesses at local hospitals. My involvement began with a young boy named Robbie and the Muscular Dystrophy Association Labor Day Telethon. Jerry Lewis began hosting the telethon in the mid-1960s, and by the 1970s, it had become a staple of American television, airing nearly twenty-four hours straight over Labor Day weekend.

The on-air show alternated between the main event, hosted by Lewis in locations like Las Vegas or NBC studios in New York, and local broadcasts featuring regional celebrities. Chuck and I participated in the regional effort for several years.

The primary shooting location for the Cleveland broadcasts was at fancy venues like Stouffer Tower City Plaza Hotel, and the show aired on WJW-TV8 for many years, hosted by Dick Goddard and other TV8 on-air talent. Chuck and I were remote correspondents, conducting events from around the city, including Public Square, outside the WJW-TV8 building, and even the SouthPark Mall in Strongsville just before it officially opened in 1996. One year, we collected so much money in our 3-foot-by-3-foot fishbowl that I had to jump in and scoop it out one bucket at a time, as we feared that lifting the bowl might crack from the weight of the coins.

One time, during the broadcast from Public Square, a kid named Robbie, who was barely able to walk and attached to an oxygen tank, dropped a jar full of change into the donation bowl and explained, "I'm in Rainbow Babies and Children's Hospital. I saw on TV that Jerry's kids needed help, so I went room to room in the hospital and collected this money." It was everything I could do to hold back the tears.

Robbie's generosity and courage had such a profound impact

on me that I began visiting him and other children at the hospital. When I started, I didn't have a clue what I was going to do, nor did I know what to expect—I just knew I wanted to do something. As I had many times before, I relied on my gut and my experience entertaining. I quickly realized I was there to offer a positive distraction from their harsh realities and a touch of normalcy they rarely experienced. Sometimes, this meant simply being there to listen. Many children had physical limitations, which affected how we could interact and what activities we could do together. Visiting never became easy, emotionally, but each visit taught me more about how I could have a positive impact. Being with those kids gave me a deep respect for their incredible bravery in facing life's toughest challenges. Witnessing their struggles was heart-wrenching, and I didn't realize how much those visits were affecting me. After returning home, I'd snap at my sons over trivial complaints, barking at them, "I just came from the hospital where kids are fighting for their lives, so I don't want to hear you whine!" The emotional weight of witnessing so much suffering clouded my ability to empathize with the everyday challenges my family faced. I didn't realize that was happening until Sherry spoke with me about it. It was hard seeing those kids suffering, but I gradually learned to manage my response to it better and not take my frustrations out on my family. Visiting these kids remains one of the most rewarding experiences of my life.

A Special Goodbye

My business partner and dear friend, Charles M. Schodowski, passed away on January 19th, 2025, which was also my birthday. How can I sum up fifty years of friendship, more than half my life, in a few short sentences?

I was honored to speak at Chuck's memorial service, a private

event for close friends and family. In the week leading up to the service, I made notes and carefully crafted what I wanted to say. But on the day of the memorial, as I was driving to the service, I realized I had left my eulogy on the kitchen table—and I was too far from home to turn around now.

For the entire time we worked together, Chuck called me every Thursday morning to remind me, "Don't forget, we're taping tonight." I always wondered why he felt the need to call, as if I would forget, which I never did. Maybe it was because he called me that I never forgot. As I continued my drive to the memorial service, I thought about those calls and wished my friend could have called one more time to remind me. As I drove on, unsettled at first that I didn't have my notes, I realized I didn't need a script to speak about someone I had known for so long. I had written the eulogy from my heart; it would be just as easy to talk from the same place.

When Chuck retired and the show ended in 2007, we called that last episode "The End of an Era." With Chuck's passing, that phrase holds an even deeper meaning. There is no arguing that

Chuck was a comedic genius, leaving an extraordinary TV legacy spanning of over sixty years, something I am grateful and proud to have been a part of.

I can't possibly summarize fifty years of friendship in a few sentences. But I can say this: The memories and the laughter we shared are endless and stay with me always. Chuck's impact on my family and me was profound. He was like a brother to me. I miss him terribly!

That's All There Is

Hey, wake up, gang! We've come to the end.

Now you've gotten the full scoop on my eighty years of life—the laughs, the misadventures, and everything in between. I hope you enjoyed reading these amusing recollections. And if you did, buy another copy and give it to a friend. After all, sharing is caring! But if you didn't, let me remind you—there are no refunds.

A friend once told me that people always smile whenever they mention my name. That is probably the best compliment I've ever received, because I genuinely believe that making people smile is why I am here.

Bye!

SPECIAL THANKS

Fans

To the fans of *The Big Chuck & Lil' John Show,* this book is as much a tribute to you as it reflects my experiences. I am grateful for how you've embraced me and for you being an essential part of my life. From the first laugh I got with Bridget the Midget to the countless others that followed, your loyal enthusiasm has made my life truly special. To this day, I'm still flattered when fans approach me in public and say, "Lil' John, I hope I'm not bothering you, but could I take a picture with you?"

I always respond, "I would be bothered if you didn't ask me to take a picture."

Don't You Guys Have Real Jobs?

While the heyday of *The Big Chuck & Lil' John Show* is behind us, the unwavering dedication of passionate fans endures. At the risk of forgetting someone, for which I ask forgiveness, I want to offer a special thank you to the following super fans who have contributed in numerous ways to keep the show's spirit alive.

C.R. Hendrix II, Chip Hess, Patrick Keeney, Robert Lazar and Jay Summers for their efforts managing the thriving Facebook group "It's The Big Chuck & Lil' John Page!"

Ron Garsteck for his years of dedication to organizing the Ghoulardifest.

Jay Summers, for his one-man operation administering the official Big Chuck & Lil' John website (bigchuckliljohn.com) and the countless hours he and C.R. have spent archiving and preserving video from the show and also gathering fan videos.

Thanks to the following individuals for their contributions of loaning their personal video recordings, which have been invaluable in preserving and archiving the show's history: Bill Ward, David "Coondog" O'Karma, David Stoner, Don Cirelli, Gary Smith, James Harmon, Janet Jay, Jim Szymanski, Jason Light, Jerry James, John Hluckey, Larry Richardson, Ryan Cousino, and Ray "King" Glasser. Your efforts will preserve the family-friendly work Chuck and I created, allowing future generations to enjoy it.

I also want to thank Kevin Salyer, a former WJW executive. He was always in our corner, supporting the show in ways big and small. Also, station employees Andy Fishman and Mark Singer supported me even after the show went off the air, inviting me back to be a special guest. Your support was genuine, and I've never forgotten it.

Friends

I couldn't end this book without mentioning a few additional close friends.

Tony Musachio I met on the show—he was the popcorn guy handing bagsful to the audience during breaks. One of the last true salesmen, he has his fingers in several businesses—all with the slogan "Everybody Knows Tony." He affectionately calls me his "Little Buddy."

Jim Carey worked for a wine company when we met and advised me never to order the house wine at a restaurant. It's poured straight from gallon-sized jugs they paid five dollars for.

Bob Ferguson has been a fan of the show since the Ghoulardi days in the 1960s and eventually became our commissioned artist

With super fans and super friends Jay Summers and Ryan Cousino, in our "certain ethnic sweaters." *(C.R. Hendrix II)*

for official show T-shirts, patches, and stickers in the 1980s. For years, he has given me a handmade figurine at Christmas, and I cherish them.

Joe Skala I met while playing against a local radio basketball team. At a towering 6′5″, I invited him to join the All-Stars team. Some fans might remember that he dressed up in a top hat and a gorilla costume, going by the name "Zipparilla."

Joe Tenebria loves to tell the story of how I insulted him the first time we met, at a Christmas party. I had picked up two small pastries, and Joe said, "Those are small; take a few more." Trying to be funny, I said, "If I take too many, I'll look like you." Despite my wisecrack, Joe and I became great friends.

I couldn't list all my friends and to those who didn't make the cut, please know your friendship means the world to me. And if you step up your game, maybe you'll make it into the next book—if there is one. Picking up the check at lunch next time is a good place to start.

Unfortunately, at my age, it's often the harsh reality of death that brings about friendship changes and sadly, some of my friends mentioned in this book are no longer alive. I miss them and often think of the great times we had.

Whether you've been a friend since early on or crossed my path along the way, thank you for all the adventures and misadventures, and for choosing to spend your time with me.

"Me Write a Book?"

Storytelling comes as naturally to me as breathing. For years, I've shared my life stories with those around me, and friends and family have repeatedly suggested that I write a book. But I've always brushed off the idea, believing it would be tedious and time-consuming, distracting me from too many other things.

However, thanks to a fortuitous introduction to C.R. Hendrix II, the idea of writing a book suddenly seemed intriguing. Despite our complete lack of combined qualifications, here it is—the book I never intended to write. C.R. spent many hours listening to me talk about myself, enduring the same question countless times: "Wait, did I already tell you this one?" Even though he has the patience of a saint—or possibly a madman—in hindsight, I should have sent over a Costco-sized bottle of Advil and a case of vodka.

C.R., I couldn't have done it without you. Well, to be honest, as you suggested, I probably could've picked a professional writer or anyone with a basic understanding of grammar. Kidding aside, I truly couldn't have chosen a better partner.

After all these months of talking with you, I've worked up quite a thirst! So, drinks are on me . . . unless it's your round. In that case, I'll have my usual: a Ketel on the rocks. On second thought, since you're buying, make mine a double—and you might as well throw in an appetizer.

ONE LAST THING...

For the pessimists or the people who read the last page first because they can't wait to see how it ends—congratulations! I wrote this page just for you. (But if you never get to the rest of the book, you're missing some pretty good stories.)

My hair is gray now (the survivors, anyway), and it's been a lifetime since I looked like the guy on the cover. But the smile? That hasn't changed. My perspective hasn't, either. Life is unpredictable, with plenty of highs and lows, but the punchline is always there if you're willing to look for it.

I still am—and always will be—laughing my way through life.

Other books of interest . . .

Big Chuck!

My Favorite Stories from 47 Years on Cleveland TV

Chuck Schodowski, Tom Feran

A beloved Cleveland TV legend tells funny and surprising stories from a lifetime in television. "Big Chuck" collaborated with Ernie Anderson on the groundbreaking "Ghoulardi" show and continued to host a late-night show across four decades—the longest such run in TV history. Packed with behind-the-scenes details about TV and celebrities.

"A vivid picture of an honest man in the insane world of television. Highly recommended." – Midwest Book Review

Ghoulardi

Inside Cleveland TV's Wildest Ride

Tom Feran, R. D. Heldenfels

The behind-the-scenes story of the outrageous Ghoulardi show and its unusual creator, Ernie Anderson. The groundbreaking late-night TV horror host shocked and delighted Northeast Ohio in the mid-1960s on Friday nights with strange beatnik humor, bad movies, and innovative sight gags. Includes rare photos, interviews, transcripts, and trivia.

"Captures a hint of the mania that made Ghoulardi a Cleveland idol in a sleepy era before long hair, drugs, assassinations, war and protests." – Columbus Dispatch

Tales from the Road

Memoirs from a Lifetime of Ohio Travel, Television, and More

Neil Zurcher

After a million miles and four decades as a TV reporter, Neil Zurcher has many great stories to tell: He met Prince Charles in a bathroom, and tripped and fell on President Gerald Ford. He raced on an elephant, piloted a glider, and hung from a trapeze. He survived a hotel fire, a tornado, and countless stunts for the camera. Fun tales well told.

"A sparkling gem of a book . . . Intermingled with the pratfalls, hijinks and practical jokes are bittersweet stories of love and romance, tragedy and triumph . . . a remarkably well-written book." – The Morning Journal

More at **www.grayco.com**

Other books of interest . . .

Six Inches of Partly Cloudy

Cleveland's Legendary TV Meteorologist Takes on Everything--and More

Dick Goddard

Legendary Cleveland TV personality and pioneering meteorologist Dick Goddard celebrates 50 years on television with this grab-bag of personal stories, witty cartoons, fun facts, and essays about weather, pets, Ohio history, the TV business, and much more. Includes favorite stories about Dick told by friends and colleagues.

Cleveland TV Tales

Stories from the Golden Age of Local Television

Mike Olszewski, Janice Olszewski

Remember when TV was just three channels and the biggest celebrities in Cleveland were a movie host named Ghoulardi, an elf named Barnaby, and a newscaster named Dorothy Fuldheim? Revisit the early days in these lively stories about the pioneering entertainers who invented television programming before our very eyes. Filled with fun details.

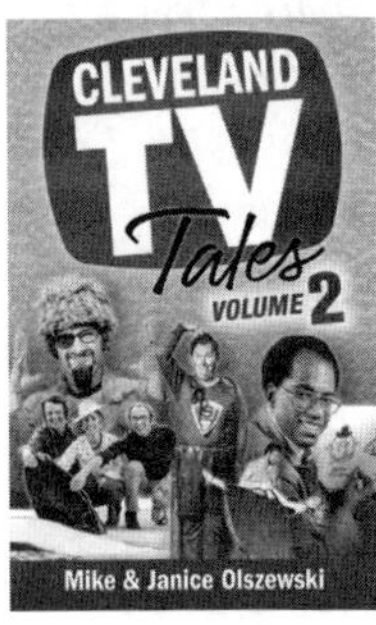

Cleveland TV Tales Volume 2

More Stories from the Golden Age of Local Television

Mike Olszewski, Janice Olszewski

More behind-the-screen stories from Cleveland TV history (1960s-'90s), including the rise of glamorous news anchors with big hair and perky noses, battling horror-movie hosts, investigative reporters stalking wrongdoers on both sides of the law, a daytime host's bizarre scandal, a mayor who co-hosted with a ventriloquist's dummy, and much more.

More at **www.grayco.com**

Other books of interest . . .

From Captain Penny to Superhost

Tales from the Golden Age of Cleveland Children's Television, 1950s–1970s

Mike Olszewski, Janice Olszewski

Children's TV in Cleveland sprang from the creative minds of actors who often made it up as they went, with few special effects but lots of imagination. Barnaby, Woodrow the Woodsman, Franz the Toymaker, Romper Room's Miss Barbara, Jungle Larry... Their impact on Northeast Ohio kids was lifelong. These stories offer a glimpse behind the plywood sets.

Barnaby and Me

Linn Sheldon

Hilarious and heartbreaking memoirs from one of the most beloved figures in Cleveland history. Linn Sheldon was a pioneering children's TV host, but offscreen he led a wild life. From a Dickensian childhood in rural Ohio to Hollywood and back, his odyssey includes celebrity, personal tragedy and self-destruction, recovery, and humor throughout.

"A revealing and hilarious look at [Sheldon's] career, which blossomed along with TV itself. The anecdotes are endless." – Sun Newspapers

The Buzzard

Inside the Glory Days of WMMS and Cleveland Rock Radio—A Memoir

John Gorman, Tom Feran

This rock and roll radio memoir goes behind the scenes at the nation's hottest station during FM's heyday, from 1973 to 1986. It was a wild and creative time. John Gorman and a small band of true believers remade rock radio while Cleveland staked its claim as the "Rock and Roll Capital." Filled with juicy insider details.

"Gorman describes in exclusive, behind-the-scenes detail the state of rock 'n' roll from the early '70s to the late '80s, when just about anything happened and everyone looked the other way . . . Essential reading for musicians, entertainment industry leaders, and music fans." – Mike Shea, CEO/Co-Founder, Alternative Press magazine

More at **www.grayco.com**

Other books of interest . . .

Lanigan in the Morning

My Life in Radio

John Lanigan

If you woke up with John Lanigan on the radio (along with hundreds of thousands of other Clevelanders), you'll enjoy the legendary jock's personal tales: the early days of talk radio; wild and dangerous publicity stunts; fierce ratings battles; interviewing movie celebs, politicians, and porn stars; hosting the Prize Movie, and lots more.

Crazy, With the Papers to Prove It

Stories About the Most Unusual, Eccentric and Outlandish People I've Known in 45 Years as a Sports Journalist

Dan Coughlin

An award-winning Cleveland sports reporter tells stories about eccentric and outlandish characters he knew in his 40-year career, including a degenerate gambler; a sportswriter who ripped open beer cans with his teeth; an Olympic champion who turned out to be a hermaphrodite; a football player who was a compulsive practical joker; and many others.

"Fascinating and fun . . . If you love Cleveland sports—in spite of the records—you will love this book." – The Morning Journal

Cleveland Food Memories

A Nostalgic Look Back at the Food We Loved, the Places We Bought It, and the People Who Made It Special

Gail Ghetia Bellamy

Remember when food was local? This book collects the fondest memories of Clevelanders who ache for favorite treats from the past. Hough Bakery. Frostees in the Higbee's basement. Popcorn balls at Euclid Beach. Burgers at Manner's or Mawby's. Entertainment-filled nights at Alpine Village. Mustard at old Municipal Stadium. And much more.

"Be prepared to be hungry, not only for your favorite foods, but for the special times from your childhood." – Currents

More at **www.grayco.com**